One Side of Suicide

Experience moving from
surviving to thriving

Dee Burt

Pen & Publish

Published by Pen & Publish
Bloomington, Indiana
(812) 837-9226
info@PenandPublish.com
www.PenandPublish.com

ISBN: 0-9768391-6-4
This book is printed on acid free paper.

Printed in the USA

Dedication

To my four children
Ross, Elizabeth, Lauren, and Alison.
I love you with all of my heart.

Acknowledgements

There have been so many people who have helped me during the writing of this book. My sincere gratitude for the part each one of you has played in my healing process. Many of you dear ones are mentioned in the following chapters. I'll do my best to honor everyone else here:

My husband, Paul, for selflessly showering me with undivided attention for long, precious stretches of time. He picked me up more times than I will ever be able to count.

My mother and father, for instilling in me a love for the healing power in words, stories, and poetry.

My brother, Mark, for his kindness, love, and being there for us.

My grandparents, for lavishing me with unconditional love and being role models demonstrating an enthusiastic thirst for knowledge and a deep sense of caring.

My Nickell family for eternal love and support.

My Burt family for helping us reclaim a joy in loving and living.

Teresa Burgin, for incredible dedication and friendship and for providing the illustrations for this book. We planned several of the illustrations while walking in the sand alongside Lake Michigan.

Min Gates, graphic artist and friend, for her humor and patience in designing this book.

Garrett Poortinga, photographer who provided photographs for cover.

Ellen Combs, for her friendship and sharing her annual visit to The Ranch, a retreat blessed with powerful women, where I stated my personal goal: to write therapeutic books and help children write books too.

Greg Hill, for friendship, insights, prayer, and healing massage.

Jeri Lucas, for her love, generosity, and healing yoga exercises and meditations.

Marsha Manning, for her friendship, family love, and heart to heart talks.

Linda Melick, for the many words of loving encouragement and wisdom shared around a campfire.

Thanks to all; family, extended family, and friends, who have walked with me. I am forever grateful for everyone in my life.

Foreword

Eighteen years have gone by since my husband ended his life. Eighteen years of confusion, reflection, and celebration of the life he led and the lives his family has to lead. Months after Nick killed himself his angry images continued to stalk me. I prayed for a peaceful night's sleep. It doesn't matter whether or not his images were dreams, terrors, guilt, or visits from the other side. They changed me. I had an eerie feeling going to bed. I closed my eyes, blinked, opened them and continued to meet his angry glare.

"Till death do us part," he charged out of clenched teeth.

Our son's eighth birthday party was doomed from the start. Nick brought home a BB gun for him and another fight ignited. "No guns!" I screened. Balloons and birthday cake filled the house while threats and fear ruined the air.

The children and I left to stay with my parents for a few days.

"Nick and I are having problems and need some time apart." Outside of the boxing ring would have been more accurate.

Late the second night the phone blared through my sleep. The usual obscenities cut through the wires and I laid the receiver down on the table. I didn't hang up. The sickness of codependence and addictive love stuck the phone back up on my ear.

"Are you there?"

Silence.

"I swear I'll kill you if you ever hang up on me. You can tell your parents to watch out too."

"What are you talking about?" I asked.

"You can't leave me. Not now. We've been through too much together. What about the kids? Don't you care if they have a dad? Or, do you already have someone lined up?"

Silence.

"Come home tonight. Alone. We need to talk. I promise I won't hurt you."

I sighed, hung up and told mom I had to go. I was just as sick as he was. Mom's eyes sank back, heavy and black. She couldn't stop the obsession. I was out of her control. She must be content with keeping her grandchildren safe.

God, what was I doing? I married him. I thought I owed him. The thirty minutes on the highway did not clear my mind. I turned the key to our little three-bedroom ranch. The night air had cooled to a perfect 68 degrees. Stars lit up the night sky and I looked around our neighborhood. There wasn't a soul awake who could help me and I walked inside.

He was waiting, naked, for me in bed. We made love that night or some sick variation of obligatory sex and solved absolutely nothing. Neither one of us knew how to get beyond ourselves. Many years later I can label the love we shared. Addictive love. The cycle of violence had circled throughout our twelve-year marriage. The honeymoon stage with chocolate hearts, red roses, and spontaneous sex flowed into the tension-building stage filled with vulgarity and insults which crashed into the explosive stage cram packed with screams, broken flower pots, and overturned bowls of chili dinners... and then? The honeymoon stage all over again, and again, and again. Memories twisted into nightmares.

Nick's eyes chased me from his grave as I trembled for the lights to turn on and scare the demons away. There had been so much fear, depression, and anger prior to our separation. I'm not leaving for someone else, I thought. I'm leaving to save my life. Selfish? Around and around the images flew, old dialogues, new additions. Exhaustion eventually awakened a willingness that brought hope for a peaceful night's sleep.

Norman Cousins once said the capacity for hope is the most significant fact of life. It provides human beings with a sense of destination and the energy to get started. I knew deep inside of me that Nick had loved each one of us and we still loved him.

One night I cuddled up all of the love I had for him, looked into his rage and held my heart up to him. Night after night love melted the icy scare of madness. Every time his eyes met mine I focused on the love that had brought us together, gave us children and brought laughter into our home. At one time, our life had fullness, excitement, and beauty. It had been much more than arguments and addictions. I offered Nick the only thing that mattered. Love. I slept.

Table of Contents

Introduction

One Side of Suicide explores life, death, love, and the challenges human beings are faced with during loss and grief. My husband staged his own death, but not his alone. The family he left behind lost a loving, passionate, talented person and still whispers his name at night. It is my sincere hope that you will find comfort in my story.

I began journaling six months after my husband's death. It was during my second semester at the university. Our first assignment in English class spread across the entire semester... complete a journal entry each day. The writings latched on to my emotions and pulled them out into plain view. My pen scrawled from page to page. It never stopped to question the content of its flow. Curled up in our La-Z-Boy, I dug up the roots of my pain. I raked over my heritage and discovered I had created myself to be a sufferer, a controller. I believed that it was my duty to suffer for Nick's father, brothers, and children as if they couldn't do it for themselves. I wanted to control life... and death. Maybe if I controlled others, no one else would feel bad enough to die. Mid-semester, my English professor offered her condolences along with an apology. She apologized for the coffee stains she left on my memoirs and thanked me for saving her from late night television. I continued to journal my anger, hatred, forgiveness and hope long after Writing Composition 101.

Our children hold individual memories of their father's suicide. My goal is to relate to you from my personal experience. However, I will share some experiences from my children's perspective. Sadly, it took several years for me to realize the mountains of hurt hidden deep within the fountain of youth. I will never know the extent of my children's grief. I had my father forty-four years.

The spiritual message in *One Side of Suicide* is to have faith in a Higher Power, Love, Intuition, Spirit, Truth, Nature. It is a non-denominational spirituality that is always open and ready to serve. Our spiritual essence requires a deep trust in the order of nature. Balance. The physical part of us requires that we nourish ourselves with healthy foods and beverages, have enough rest and exercise to keep ourselves limber and mobile. Our minds require information before decisions can be made. Logic, at times, pulled me away from guilt and out of the past more directly than prayer and push-ups.

It is up to us to search for sources to achieve peace of mind. We are more than our minds, more than our bodies, and more than our spirits. It is my goal to honor the mystery of life within and around everyone more reverently than ever before. Nick's short time on earth will live on because the legend of love is eternal. The same is true for your loved one. Let us move forward to realize our potential to thrive. We can use the freedom of choice that Nature so freely gave us to design our self-care plan. Dr. Jampolsky offers us the challenge and invitation to imagine waking up and feeling perfectly happy, peaceful, and loving in his book, *Love Is Letting Go Of Fear*. He states that all of this is possible when our forgiveness is complete.

Healing is possible for all who are ready and willing to let go of judgment and love themselves through their anger, fear, and pain. The grieving process has no exact timetable, but it does have a mix of the following unique stages: (1) shock, (2) denial and isolation, (3) relief, (4) depression, (5) guilt, (6) anger, (7) bargaining, (8) forgiveness, and (9) acceptance, and hope. Survivors of suicide add an extra load of guilt to the grieving process, guilt that is periodically dumped and continuously sprinkled throughout the entire process. Acceptance comes in waves and washes away the final sands of guilt.

This book follows a bereavement-based format. The first stage, shock, literally catches a person off guard and places him or her into a state of wide-eyed denial or shut-eyed numbness. The reality is just too horrifying at that point to believe or deal with.

The second stage, denial allows the mind and body to isolate and wait for subtle signs of life and readiness. The mind begins to question. What happened? Why? We poke around our loved one's favorite spots and come back empty handed, alone.

Awareness grabs hold of us and guides us into the third stage, relief or catharsis. I felt relief because I had been afraid of my husband's anger. Now, his anger was dead. Sobs purged and dehydrated me after shock. The residue after catharsis was deep, dry sadness.

The fourth stage, depression, pointed to the facts: his name in the obituaries, the memorial Bible, his body hidden... was it in the casket? Intellectually, I accepted the fact that he was dead and that life changed. This stage lingers for days, months, or even years if one tries to get around it rather than go through it. Depression is the motivation behind this book. Survivors who try to avoid sadness and self-expression can remain depressed for lifetimes. Some survivors become victims during clinical depression and choose to end their lives as well. The pain seems unbearable, inescapable.

The fifth stage, guilt, rakes spouses, brothers and sisters, sons and daughters, parents and friends over the coals of hell. Survivors ask, "What could I have done?" Hindsight often provides options that are no longer possibilities. Thoughts that increase guilt are best laid to rest.

The sixth stage, anger, just about conquered my mind and tossed it off the planet. Would my anger be the death of me too?

A soft-spoken minister told me to rejoice, "Anger is the most natural stage of all. Get angry and you will survive."

The seventh stage, bargaining, is the hit or miss stage. It is like the sniper who sneaks around your brain's backyard and shoots in pathetic little ideas such as, "Tell God you'll surrender your life to the mission of world peace, homelessness, illiteracy anything," to undo the suicide. I experienced times when the reality was so sad, sick, or sadistic that I would dream up some little story. Nick, alive and alert, pacing around in his workshop with a wrench in his back pocket and a transmission spread out on the floor... waiting for his script to play on. Yes, grief can be postponed. Bargaining jumps around in and out of the other stages as the intensity mounts.

The eighth stage, forgiveness, opens up our hearts to hopes and dreams for a future and leads us into the last stage.
Acceptance, allows you to cherish the one who died and respect the life you have left to live.

Your life may be standing still for the first time. Look inside and discover your truth. Peace of mind will follow. Today's roadblocks are the foundational steps laid to support a rich new journey. Right now if you want to throw this book out of the window, stop! Eighteen years ago I could not imagine happiness ever hugging me again. Happiness comes to a place prepared to sustain it. May you open your side of the suicide to feelings and thoughts that nurture you.

Throughout this book questions and journal invitations are presented to initiate self-examination. Take note of your feelings when you read each one for the first time. Be prepared to record these feelings in words or illustrations without judging them as right or wrong. Your feelings are your inner traffic lights signaling you to get moving, slow down, breathe, or exhale.

Why a workbook? You picked up this book because now is the time for additional emotional work. Eleven years ago I noticed that my daily, involuntary thoughts of Nick stopped. I was caught up in life; running and playing with our children again, graduation from university, planting flowers; cultivating life.

This book is an experiential workbook. The reader feels. The reader writes. You will explore your side of suicide and facilitate your personal "grief-to-peace" course.

We are complex beings in a complex world. The world will go right on spinning even if we choose to cement ourselves to the past. If we are to make sense of the world within and around us, we must come to terms with our whole being: spiritual, physical, and mental. Soul, body and mind work together throughout the grieving process. I invite you to explore these aspects, as you are ready.

The writing of this book has been a healing journey. Each sentence helped me process as I hope it helps you. I plan to give each one of our beautiful, thriving children a copy. Yes, I have been afraid that they would uncover my flaws and connect the dots to Nick's demise. Yet, I've walked all over each and every dot and know in my heart my intention was not to harm him.

Take an honest inventory of what is weighting you down. It takes a lot of work to write, draw, walk, and crawl through our feelings in our quest for peace. Unexpressed emotion can create headaches, depression and disease, but it does not have to plague our spirits forever. Allow yourself the time and space for mental and emotional cleansing. Are you willing to begin the unraveling process? It doesn't matter that your life may be a ball of confusion at this point in time. We don't unwind at the same rate nor must we analyze each string of the past before we begin our self-healing work.

Throughout this book I encourage you to trust your feelings. Feelings indicate where you are emotionally. Be alert to their purpose. Feelings make us conscious of an inward impulse, state of mind, or a physical condition. Awareness of feelings is an ongoing introspective lesson with at least three important steps to master:

1. Allow yourself to feel. Be. Sit with them. Welcome them. Embrace them. You are getting acquainted with the real you.

2. Identify what feeling(s) you are experiencing.

3. Ask for help to express your feelings healthfully.

The vast miracle within will nudge you with creative answers. There were times I was too angry to sit, speak, write, or scribble. Instead, I picked up walnuts and threw them into a blur of tulip poplars, maples, and hard oaks. Each throw honored one part of beat-skipping rage. You'll get ideas. I look back and am grateful I didn't tell myself to sit down and shut up.

Preface

Scenes of our last encounter seared into my mind's eye. Nick sat cross-legged on the curb, police officers dotted the yard, and neighbors watched with babies in their arms. They used to honk and wave at him fixing our car, building patio furniture, or seeding the lawn. But that day they just stared. I rolled away with our children: Ross, Elizabeth, Lauren, and our dog, KD.

"I think we should leave KD home to keep Daddy company," insisted Ross. KD had slept with Ross for six solid years. It was the most generous gift he had to offer... his dog to watch over his dad. I locked my eyes on the road and drove on. Hours later we pulled into an Econo Lodge. The five of us squeezed together on one king sized bed.

Finally safe I dialed my parents. Dad answered on the first ring. "Thank God. You're all right," he cracked.

I left Nick. He loved us dearly. This man I loved, feared, and resented. We would bury him two short weeks later.

I woke up to the sleeping sounds of our children and thought about the day before that brought us to the motel. Nick's jaw locked tight when I read his apology card. My shoulders stiffened. I no longer cared how sorry he was. The marriage was over. I watched the muscles in his cheeks ripple as he ground his teeth together. He gathered up the children, his three and the little ones in my day care. I picked the baby up and held her on my lap.

"Come on curly top," he said. "Everyone stay in the playroom and don't come out," he ordered. Nick had never laid a violent hand on his children.

"What should I do?" my mind raced.

Nick paced, "Bitch. You're so cold. We have three kids. I hate your fucking guts." The room echoed hatred off of the four thin walls. Brittany sucked her bottle and I laid her in the large wooden playpen in the family room. I turned to the patio doors with Nick's breath on the back of my neck.

"Say something. Hit me," he rasped. Two neighbors were stretched out on a quilt on the other side of the fence we shared. Thank God. I'm not alone.

Nick's stifled rage saturated the wet July air. His step was brisk as he waved at them.

Ross popped his head out the door and asked, "Can we come out now, Daddy?"

"No." Nick marched his worried son back to isolation.

I moved quickly to the fence. "If you see anything bad call the police." They sipped their tea, talked, and sat... stationed on their blanket.

Nick returned, "Come inside. Now!" I shook my head and rooted myself in the lawn. He moved close and wrapped my hair around one hand and cupped the other one over my mouth.

"Go inside, damn it." I followed him to hell like an unwilling dog on a short leash. My brain throbbed with raw, sudden pain as he ripped out a handful of hair. That was my neighbor's cue and she dialed the police. Nick dragged me indoors and across the living room floor.

Why had we succumbed to such violent sickness? Fear can kill a person just as tragically as a bullet or a belt or a bump on the brain. I hated myself for being afraid. I hated him for all of the threats. I scrambled up onto the sofa next to the window. The screen checked the blue-white sky. I wished I could run, but drew my bare legs up in front of me. He picked on my left thigh and started pounding one blow after the other with his rock hard fist... if my leg broke I would be stuck.

"I'm not afraid to die. We're already living in hell," he ranted.

Ross showed up one more time with big, green saucer eyes. "Daddy?"

Nick turned and shouted questions. "Am I hurting her? Am I doing anything wrong? What's wrong?" Ross just stared and shook his head from side to side. Next, it bobbed slightly up and down. His son was silent.

An arrow of sunlight sneaked through the living room door. Some little someone had left it ajar again. I darted outside. Nick, a few paces behind shoved me to the ground just as the police pulled to a stop. My dear friend Marsha cared for my daycare children as I packed Ross, Elizabeth, Lauren, and the dog in our little hatchback.

Daily a plan to permanently separate developed and died inside of my mind. Another friend, Suzanne rescued me from my confusion, desperation, and indecision. She knew I would go back to him eventually if he found me, coerced me, and seduced me. Suzanne blessed me with friendship and unconditional love. She confided in me that she too had been on the receiving end of emotional abuse and was preparing to leave her husband. The difference between us was power and insight. Suzanne prepared a safe haven for herself and purchased a large, lovely brick home in a quiet neighborhood. It stood empty as she waited for the appropriate time to leave her spouse. The children and I moved in the very next day and left no forwarding address or telephone number with anyone. Suzanne called my parents and told them we were being well cared for and not to worry.

Memories plagued the nights in our hideout. "You'll be sorry. I hope you find someone more like your own self to drive you crazy!" His rage bellowed inside of my head as I tucked Ross, Elizabeth, and Lauren into their temporary beds.

Nick learned quickly that no one knew where we were. He lost contact with the only true security he had known in a long time. His family vanished overnight.

Journal

Write or draw about:

· **What may happen in your life if you decide to throw this book out of the window?**

· **What may happen in your life if you use this book and record your feelings?**

Chapter 1

Scattered Notes

**We cannot look at the sun all the time,
we cannot face death all the time.**

Elisabeth Kubler-Ross

Where did he go? The light was on next to his chair. The radio sang. The house was empty. I discovered the truth behind his absence scratched on white notepaper scattered across grandma's old canning table. He was thirty-two years old and signed his last words, "No Need, Nick." He had drawn a circle with two dots for eyes, no nose, a straight line for a mouth next to his name. No smile, no frown, no expression. My friend pieced the puzzle together and sent her husband out in search of his body. Nick's garage reeked with the smell of his remains, which were slumped over the steering wheel of his Camero. He had stretched an air compressor hose from the exhaust pipe through the driver's window and clamped it into place.

People die on battlefields fighting in the name of peace, in their own beds desperately gasping for a miracle cure, while others take their own lives before they know whom they truly are. Suicide is a wretched waste.

I was tempted to tell our children that their daddy died in a car accident. My denial and isolation began as I tried to rescue our children before the lightening bolt of their father's suicide could hit them. Did I want to protect us from the stigma attached to a survivor of suicide or pretend that his death occurred under more common circumstances? The masquerade could never last. I wondered about the outcome when time revealed we had lived a lie. Children instinctively know when there is more to a story. Grown ups lower their voices while children lock their eyes to their lips, brows, and body language. My fingers caressed his last words folded into a square in my pocket. I couldn't lie to our children. The car accident detour would have rationed out filthy guilt over a precious lifetime.

My mind raced for explanations of his absence. Denial was truly a buffer and played tricks with my eyes. The suntan lotion sitting with the lid half opened jolted my mind about half a click, but I passed it by. I checked the patio, the bedroom, the bathroom and expected to find him alive... rinsing his hands, eyes twinkling; a bad joke. I wanted to scream with delight to my little ones, "Here he is; it's OK; everything's fine!"

The trauma hadn't blistered but it had started to sting. Ross and Elizabeth looked up to me for answers. A friend held Lauren. "What could I have done; why hadn't I known; was I to blame?" I wanted to fly away, but I had to stand on hated truth. He died on purpose. Once the truth was out, it could not be retrieved or reinvented. A lie would be an agreement to live in shame. A survivor of suicide doesn't need to deal with any more shame. Shame kills too.

I went cold in the midst of a sticky, summer eve. Carbon monoxide poisoning. I looked into three sets of innocent eyes; one green like mine, another brown like grandma's, and another blue like his.

"Daddy killed himself with car smoke. He died in the garage." He left an eight-year-old son, a five-year-old daughter, and a one-year-old daughter. We watched the ambulance open up and swallow their daddy all zipped up in a man-sized plastic bag.

Policemen questioned me until my head split.
"Was your husband depressed, under medication? Was he angry?" The questions asked at the scene pierced my numb brain. "Was he allergic to anything?" "Was he allergic?" "Could he still have a pulse?" The officers finally left me alone. Our minister arrived with his wife, my psychotherapist. She counseled me on several occasions during the separation. We held hands in our neighbor's house on the hill overlooking ours. Together we formed a circle. No beginning, no end, we bowed our heads.

"Dear Father, hold Nick's spirit in everlasting love. Amen." Everyone held his or her own prayer that night.

The children and I spent the night with my parents. Questions continued to torture my mind. As parents we have a multitude of decisions to make regarding the rearing of children. We love our children and want to shelter them from life's injustices. I have never regretted telling our children the truth even though Ross responded with, "I should have helped him. I should have taken him to a doctor." Children responsible for their parents? My God, I thought it was the other way around. Children are willing to fall heir to their parents' mistakes. My son felt he could have provided the missing link, a trip to the doctor and prevented his father's suicide. But, his dad had refused both counseling and Alcoholics Anonymous. "I don't need counseling, and I don't have a drinking problem!"

I regret my abrupt disposal of snapshots and the distance I placed between his friends, his family, and me. I trashed a photo album overflowing with Harley Davidson adventures and late adolescence. I loved riding along the coastal highway with my arms hugging his warm, trim waist... summer tanning our backs. The wind whipped his sun-bleached hair and wrapped it around the molding of his candy-apple red helmet. We were invincible and soared like eagles with the spirit of companionship beneath our wings. He was gone. I wanted him to roll his fingers around the handle grips and ride again. Instead, another handful of snapshot memories fell into the trashcan. What was I afraid of? He wouldn't jump off of the prints and attack me. Now, our children won't have many pictures of their dad.

Nick made toys for his children, painted friends' homes, and fixed their radiators and transmissions. He comforted them when their relationships trickled down the tubes. He held me in his arms when a car hit Elizabeth. He calmed me down, stopped me from spitting in the face of the negligent driver. On my side of suicide, guilt bubbled up like hot oil and splattered flashbacks on the promise of each new day. Anxiety grabbed onto my shoulders and shook me. I couldn't forget the goodness and love with which he had showered me.

I was angry and afraid. I had pretended for years that I could handle anything. I hid my sorrow from our children each time Nick and I fought. I would pack them up and drive to the Children's Museum, twenty short minutes away. Sometimes I would call home to check his temperament. Was he still angry or had he slept it off? The answer would determine whether or not we would share supper at the table with daddy or have McDonald's Happy Meals. He didn't drink at home, much anyway, I lied to myself. The children didn't see the bottles he consumed between 7 o'clock in the morning and noon. He worked the graveyard shift and needed something to calm him down, sedate him, so he could sleep while the rest of the neighborhood played. He used to pull in the driveway and walk straight to his workshop with plans for a giant sandbox, jungle gym, or backyard swing. He loved to play. Ross and Elizabeth would find him building their newest toy from scratch. We still have those little wooden soldiers with tiny metal washer buttons down their fronts. He helped the children paint their initials on the backs. He sawed and nailed and hoisted fifty-pound bags of clean, white sand on top of his broad shoulders, whistling, all the way to their sturdy new sandbox.

What happened to the love we once shared? Why had I pretended to agree with him, to enjoy him, to love him? Nick used to ask me to join him for a whiskey sour like in the good ole days. I used to eat the orange and chew up the maraschino cherry before guzzling down my favorite drink.

The arguments we used to get into after those drinks stopped me from ordering them. I became a poised prude. He would be high. High on life itself or beer or something and I would stare right through his joy with cold, solemn eyes.

The arguments didn't stop but their themes changed. Now, it was his drinking that caused all of our problems. I no longer drank and was innocent as a wide-eyed child. It would be years before I understood how and why I enabled him. I looked down at our babies' faces on the night the ambulance consumed Nick and prayed they would forgive me for the lies I slipped into their daddy's soul.

Our minister, Nick's father and brother planned the funeral with me nodding in agreement between them. We played Bridge Over Troubled Waters and Morning Has Broken. A dear friend from high school sang Morning Has Broken with her golden voice at our wedding twelve years earlier. The chapel we created inside of my parents' living room vibrated with hope and happiness for a long, happy life together.

During the funeral, I sat off to the side propped up against my brother's shoulder. He protected me through the service with the love and kindness I desperately needed. I knew he didn't blame me.

"Sis, Nick was threatened by you. It wasn't your fault." The polished brown casket was closed. My neighbor saw him last. Mom thought she talked to him last. Our family portrait smiled on an easel and faced a parlor full of family and friends. My thoughts raced as I relived the day we had that portrait made.

Nick's mother asked us from her deathbed to have it made. She was eaten up with cancer, and I would not refuse her.

I kept our marital problems a secret. We swept our broken dreams under the rug, sat our children on our laps, and smiled for the photographer. This is the last portrait I'll make with Nick, I vowed to myself as the camera snapped and flashed.

So many hearts were hurt in my search for freedom. His mother had known him so well. She died two months ahead of him. Had she not wanted to mourn her first-born son? Perhaps she hastened on ahead to prepare for him.

Three months after Nick's death came October. Halloween decorations were plastered all over town. Cold chills spread up and down my body. I stared, trancelike, at dangling dead limbs. Is that what he is now? I contemplated his ghost cutting circles around our house. Nick's family had always hosted great Halloween parties. They defeated the scar of death by acting it out. One by one, his aunts, uncles, and cousins descended on Grandma and Grandpa's cow pasture. The cows were long gone but the ambience of a deserted meadow framed a headless horseman, vampires, and a variety of spooks.

One year, Nick built a set of stilts and towered above all of the little ghouls and goblins. He made a smaller set of stilts for Ross and Elizabeth and taught them how to walk just a little bit taller. I stopped attending family parties after his death. He fell over the edge of no return, and I slipped out of sight too.

The New Year passed with the conclusion that we were all skeletons wearing temporary flesh. We would all die... something I had known all of my life, but had never stopped to think about what death meant. I felt robbed.

Nature whittles away at our bones and cells until old age, terminal illness, or an accident separates spirit from a worn-out temple. Is there really a time for suicide? I pray there isn't. It is my hope that individuals will consider every option available and choose life over death. What meaning would you like to leave about your meanderings?

Elisabeth Kubler-Ross wrote about her loss and grief workshops in her book, *On Death and Dying.* She described the following five stages of grief: denial, anger, bargaining, depression, and acceptance. To graduate from the denial stage survivors are encouraged to feel the good-bye ceremony. Countless good-byes will appear around every future corner if the funeral did not implant the fact of death into your mind. We may numb and isolate ourselves in denial but memory chases us. Mourners shuffle around the funeral parlor, file into their cars, and follow purple flags stuck on shiny black cars. There is not one thing we can do to change history.

Here is an exercise for you to do if you missed the burial service of your loved one. Go outside, pick up a clump of soil and crumble it over your garden. When you are ready, bid one last formal good-bye.

Journal

Write or draw about:

· **How do you feel about life now?**

Journal

Write or draw about:

· **What conversation or scene twists and plummets inside of you?**

Journal

Write or draw about:

· **What were you thinking and feeling during the funeral service?**

· **What did you like about the service?**

· **What disappointed you about the service?**

Chapter 2

Beyond Condolences

**For everything that is given something is taken.
Nothing can bring you peace but yourself.**

Ralph Waldo Emerson

There is always a "morning after." The morning after I learned of my husband's suicide I woke up before daybreak in my childhood home.

The night before my mother and father went through the motions, "We're so very sorry. Would you like some soup? Extra blankets are in the closet." On and on... they were stunned. My father had not cried before that night. Nick's death opened the dam.

The house was dark. I slipped passed my parent's bedroom in the middle of the night and questioned myself, Was Nick really dead? I wove around furniture, out the glass doors and onto the cracked patio Dad and I had poured so many years before. Mom's rose garden held the bones of Easter ducklings and childhood treasures. Slowly, I moved past fruit trees, forsythia, and a harbor of concord grapes. My grandparents died of old age and illness after living together in marriage for fifty years. Fifty years! I used to wait on their front porch a minute or so before tapping my arrival just so I could watch them through the curtains. Grandpa in his rocking chair watched baseball. Grandma on the sofa played solitaire. Why did my husband kill himself?

Mom's sweet mint sprawled out onto a thick green turf that sprung forth with life. I stood face to face with a steel pole on which hung the first punching bag I had ever known. Over and over my fist pounded the tether ball. Over and over I screamed why. Why, God, did he do it? I wondered how anyone could still love me. Nick's mother intuitively advised us from her cancer bed, "Talk things over. Don't go to bed angry with each other."

My hands and knuckles were red and sore; anger consumed me. I felt rejected and abandoned. He was gone and I hated myself. Stretched out on the moist grass I looked up to the dawn lit sky. My eyes traveled from cloud to cloud. How long would sadness anchor my soul? How long before peace of mind would find me? Would I ever forgive myself for leaving him? Would I ever forgive him for leaving us? A flock of birds stole my attention as they lined up on a telephone wire. How long must I bear the pain?

Birds flew away. One, two, three at a time, until one bird rested alone. It sat, attached to the wire for an eternity.

Bereavement would creep. What else did I expect? I had spent my life packing feelings away until I forgot they even existed. Numbness, I knew. Did it take this sudden, tragic death to wake me up to my own walking death? Simultaneously, I protested and sought an easy way out. I watched the lonely bird and whispered to it as it flew away, I will scrub each and every cell of my being clean and free of self-pity. I walked away with the thought that self-pity clogs the very breath out of life. It is the cancer of the human soul.

I took refuge on the living room sofa and covered my face with pillows. Maybe someone would come along and snuff out my light. Oddly, self-pity was my first awkward step toward feeling. It forced me to acknowledge the depth of my hurt. Today I am grateful for the pity, and I am doubly glad it's gone. Self-pity may not be the ideal beginning of bereavement, but it can help us bend, fall down, beg a hand and stand back up. Dr. Scott Peck in, *I'm Not O.K. and You're Not O.K. and That's O.K.*, suggested that we accept all of our so-called frailties. So be it.

The grieving process sucked me down in a cesspool of anger and guilt before self-correction began. How do we survive the anger that erupts after a loss from suicide? Own it. Whether we attack others or ourselves with angry accusations, the anger belongs to us. We experience the bitter remorse of it all. Individually, we must be responsible for our feelings and expressions of anger.

I was angry because Nick wasn't here to blame for my problems anymore. I was physically free from his impulsivity and overwhelmed with my own. There were times I wanted to run off the face of the earth. Other times I curled up in his favorite chair and let tears wear long lines down my face. We had bought the chair just before Elizabeth was born. He wanted me to be cuddled in soft support as I nursed her. Nick used to sit on the arm of it and watch Elizabeth dig her toes into my soft belly. He placed his pinky inside her tiny hand and twinkled when she squeezed it. I rediscovered a love for him. My sadness was as much for the love I had rekindled as it was for the love that had decayed. Writing was a way I could touch the love I felt for him.

Denial functions as a buffer after unexpected shock. We need time to adjust to the hardness, the shivering coldness. So, whatever happened didn't really happen. We're held in a state of emotional numbness until we can deal with the tragic news. Mentally we chew up each experience leading to the death and later mix those with the discovery of the deceased, the funeral, the emptiness and plod along.

Journal

Write or draw about:

· **What is seething on your side of suicide?**

Chapter 3

Punish Me God

To accuse others for one's misfortunes is a sign of want of education.
To accuse oneself shows that one's education has begun.
To accuse neither oneself nor others shows one's education is complete.

Epictetus

Epictetus was a Stoic philosopher who believed people should focus on things they could control and not on things that were out of their control. Difficult? Blame is a curse we cast upon ourselves as we wait to be charged with neglect. Well, they just don't get it do they? Someone or something must be at fault. We either pin ourselves with a badge scratched with the words, "It's all my fault," or search for a scapegoat to run with a burning banner of blame.

Someone should have prevented the suicide: spouses, doctors, teachers, friends, enemies, relatives, or therapists. We excuse the suicide victims because they sacrificed life to express their pain. We seek and find reasons to validate our guilt and shrink under the notion of naming the deceased responsible for his or her decision to die.

Blame won't heal a broken heart. We torture ourselves when we continue to be unforgiving. Physical diseases such as insomnia, migraine headaches, ulcers, colitis, heart attacks, exhaustion, phobias, and substance abuse can attack a depleted, depressed person. Survivors who hold onto guilt push their grief work aside. Have you noticed any of the following set-ups for failure: quitting jobs, being fired, ending positive relationships abrutly, and/or considering suicide as a solution for your own pain? These are punishments for something you did not do. You did not do it. You are not responsible, but the responsibility to begin the grief work is yours. The grief work that you complete is your legacy.

Two weeks after Nick died I found an angel in the body of a high school student in our neighborhood park. Janelle watched Ross climb trees and Elizabeth push Lauren in the baby swing and asked if I needed a baby-sitter. We talked about family and friends we had in common and set a date for the five of us to ride bikes together. She was taller than me and had big blue eyes that saw right through my sadness. Her wide friendly smile confirmed my basic belief that teenagers were a compassionate, loyal people. I think it was love at first sight. She became our camp counselor who always had a fun game to play, a Disney theme song to sing, M&M's in her pocket and a video in her purse. We love her to this day.

Janelle baby-sat on nights I attended Attitudinal Healing (AH) meetings and on weekends when I shopped alone or went out for dinner with friends. AH was a support group for people who were dealing with a crisis or a stressful situation. One of my favorite principles from Attitudinal Healing is: We are never upset for the reason we think. It took several months to internalize the meaning behind such a profound statement. Prior to Attitudinal Healing I thought my anger was due to Nick's attitude and behavior. Now, I know I was mad at myself for pretending that it would get better.

The day I packed up the kids with a picnic and drove away I knew that anger was due to one thing. I couldn't control him. The problem expanded as my addiction to enable him grew. It was as debilitating as alcoholism. Why? Why? Why? Because you failed him, I answered. Nick was insecure. I had moved away from his interests. Several years prior to the birth of our children I poured a glass of rum-spiked punch left over from a party the night before. A question popped into my mind, "If I drink in the afternoon will I become an alcoholic?" I instantly made the commitment to push away from quick fixes. Instead, I obsessed on broccoli, books, and aerobics. I shopped at health food stores and whipped up homemade mayonnaise. He watched, complained, and worried. "Who are you?" he demanded.

Little by little, as my physical, mental, and emotional health improved, he crawled further down into a bottle of beer. Together we denied his alcoholism. Don't make waves. Sound familiar? A lake can be smooth as glass one minute, choppy and fatal in the next. I reached a point where I no longer accepted the facade that things were placid. We didn't know how to set boundaries much less stand by them. This lack of communication pointed to some of my sickest behaviors that had helped him sidestep rehabilitation.

Christopher Lucas and Henry Seiden wrote, *In Silent Grief* that the saddest bargain a survivor can make is: because you died, I'll die. Victims of suicide often want to sever themselves from pain from which they see no way out; survivors sometimes choose to avoid pain through the postponement of it. We bargain to be better people and hope the sadness can be lifted by the grace of God. A chorus composed itself inside my head. "Let me help this world become a better place. Let me help those with whom I race. Let me... so myself I can face." Over and over we make deals with a higher being. Deliver me from this hell and I will change. Somehow, I will change. Bargaining is a survival technique to relieve guilt. Guilt can be dissolved when the survivor blames no one for the death. There is no one to blame, not even the deceased.

I am free from the leftover survivor-of-suicide-guilt after years of playing out a million scenarios that convicted me. I have worked with children and families who also survived losses. Yet, that is not what relieved my guilt. My core nature revealed that I lied to him because I was cowardly, afraid to confront the inevitable truth that we had grown apart. Honest, forthright communication was an unfamiliar tool. I let go of guilt because my intention was never to hurt him.

I wanted to save our family from self-destruction and realized it would not happen beneath a shared roof. I left him sitting on that curb in late July because I was no longer safe with him. I let the guilt leak out of my mind, body and soul to fill in the hungry cracks of the world.

The guilt pushed me to grow and develop an improved style of communication that focused on self-responsibility and honest disclosure. I still deny problems to avoid a conflict, still bargain for a longer stretch of pretend quiet time, but just not as much as I used to.

Whatever you may bargain for, know it is temporary. If it turns an unwanted habit into a mission with honor, so be it. Just don't let it fool you into thinking that sacrifice will bring you forgiveness and peace of mind. Forgive. Forgiveness soothes your heart, mind, and soul.

Journal

Write or draw about:

· **Have you made a bargain?**

Journal

Chapter 4

Down in the Dumps

When we want to be something other than the thing God wants us to be, we must be wanting what, in fact, will not make us happy.

C.S. Lewis

Nick experienced depression alone, as many people do. Why is it during the times of greatest need that people unhook their lifelines and leave themselves disconnected? Nick sliced his connections before he killed his breath. There were many times during our marriage when his behavior screamed for help and scared it away at the same time. People push help out the door, with phrases such as, "Go away! Leave me alone! You don't care!" Others dissolve help quietly with sullen, simmering moodiness. Family and friends walk away in unsettled torment. Nick tucked himself into bed or jammed himself into a crowded club, but his call for help rang in our vacant house.

Where can a worried soul go for peace of mind? The obvious resources include: counselors, friends, family members, churches, synagogues, temples, beaches, forests, and neighbors. Nick and I didn't discuss the possibilities. Was I too busy pretending perfection to outline options for a better relationship?

One day Nick joined me in church. "How can people with so many problems be happy? This place is full of sad people just faking happiness," he said. He stayed for the music, but I could feel his uneasiness mount. I dragged him to church for an impossible quick fix, and he resented it. Locked in his pain, Nick stood up and walked out on the sermon. He was honest about his beliefs as I waited in silence for the service to end. We picked up the children from their Sunday school classes and drove home tired and weary from another public display of dysfunction. Somewhere on the road between church and home he started humming one of the hymns. This time I was scared. What if he really did change and I still couldn't stay with him? I was such a liar. I kept my fear to myself and listened. His plea for help would later choke in his throat like dry meat, and I would have to face my lack of honest communication.

Nick was a thrill-seeker who never wanted a fun-filled day or night to end. His actions seemed to say, "I'll prove the idiot who said, all good things must come to an end wrong." He would stay up all night to replace one more bolt, keep a campfire burning or admire a newly restored, freshly painted, automobile. I can still hear him whistle as he marched around in his workshop, a man with a mission in the midst of creativity. His friends called him "ruler eyes" because his measurements and calculations were flawless. When he was idle, he was depressed.

He had a laugh that would start way down in his belly, bubble up, and electrify an entire banquet hall or liven up a backyard barbecue. He extended his handyman help to family at the drop of a hat or labor over a friend's project without a glance at his watch. Happy times became fewer and frowns more frequent.

"Had a bad day. I'll be late tonight," he apologized. Depression? The good times that he lived for became a casualty of overtime, responsibilities, and resentment. They were squeezed out of his day, day after day. Did a silent guilt rage inside of Nick's head? Was suicide his only reprieve from a guilt that convinced him of his unworthiness? How long had he believed that he deserved the ultimate punishment? Did he scream for understanding, yet find those around him too scared of his wrath to respond? His reasons are not for me to judge. Months and years went by before it occurred to me that I didn't have to know why.

What about those sad, constant thoughts? I'd like to erase the soul-stripping ones and get to forgiveness, but grief doesn't work that way. Amnesia is rare. How shall we cope with depression? Every minute of my time was saturated with thoughts surrounding Nick's death. Obsessed with uncovering the "whole truth" behind his choice to die I listed violations that held me accountable for Nick's pain, sadness, anger, lack of energy, and impulsivity. My inward relentless anger and guilt caved into depression.

Depression robbed me of my ability to make ordinary decisions, participate in daily routines, and cope with stress. I was afraid that failure would strike again. The lack of self-trust weakens our ability to formulate healthy alternatives.

Slouched on the sofa surrounded by a sloppy living room, paranoia jerked me when I heard a tap on the front door. My dear friend, Marsha sat down beside Lauren and patted her little head full of sticky, uncombed hair. Marsha hugged me, talked me into a better mood, and carried my baby across the street to her house. Later that afternoon she brought back a rosy cheeked, freshly bathed, cheerful little sweetheart. She didn't judge me for neglecting to bathe my child that day.

Rest. Turn off your alarm clock and snuggle gently back into life. Allow a legacy of hope and dignity to revive the survivors. Take it one step at a time and honor simple treasures. Walk. Step to a softer melody, sing, hum, and breathe... deeply. Something positive will drift into your mind and heart for you to follow. Act on it. The depression will evaporate like the sweat on your brow.

Lukas and Seidan acknowledge in, *Silent Grief*, that post-traumatic stress disorder (PTSD) is common after experiencing a psychological trauma. Sufferers of the disorder are not crazy, but they are disturbed. Survivors, be alert to any times that you have recollections of the suicide. You may have dreams or feel like the event is happening for the first time. Sleep disturbances, guilt or anxiety about surviving, and memory loss are symptoms of post-traumatic stress disorder and should be checked out with your family doctor. It is possible and probable that you will experience a lack of interest in sports or activities that you used to enjoy. However, if a flat, emotionless feeling overcomes you, please seek some extra help in working through it. You do not have to do this alone.

Symptoms such as memory loss and underlying anxiety or paranoia can show up immediately or lay dormant for months or years. It is up to the survivor to determine how long they last. Mine prevailed for several years and didn't fully subside until I finished the first draft of this book. Your journal will aid the cleansing of your loving heart and help to set it free.

We frequently hear someone exclaim, "I saw my life pass before my eyes," after a brush with disaster. Will each one of us face a "life-review" after our heart stops beating and our blood stops flowing? Will we observe a life generated by fear or one led by love? Will we evaluate pitiful rationalizations for bridges uncrossed or jumped from, or will we rejoice with our arms lifted in triumph for the tasks we accepted? Do you have to wait for the moment between physical life and physical death before you muster up the courage to strap on your pack and climb the mountain of transformation? No one transforms us. We decide if and when we will embark upon the journey to thrive.

Journal

Write or draw about:

· **Reflect upon any stressful feelings you experience.**

Journal

Write or draw about:

· **Write about the grief that is waiting for your loving attention.**

Chapter 5

Band-Aids Won't Stick

Ask, and it shall be given to you; seek, and you shall find; knock and it shall be opened to you. For whoever asks, receives; and he who seeks, finds; and to him who knocks, the door is opened.

Matthew 7:7-11

Alice, my therapist, and I met several times during my two-week separation from Nick prior to his suicide. We continued our sessions every week for several months after the funeral. Suicidal thoughts trespassed my brain. One Saturday morning unable to climb out of bed I reached for the telephone to call Alice. My voice was hoarse, yet I had no cold or sore throat. Who or what had taken over my body? She told me to get up, get dressed, and do something. Sick and furious I pushed the suffocating pile of covers off of me, dumped them onto the floor, stood up, and grabbed my clothes.

I was mad at myself just like Nick had been mad at himself. The trouble was, when he dished his anger out on my plate, I gobbled it up and felt it stagnate in the pit of my stomach. A sick hunger within me searched for crumbs of blame and guilt. Had I recognized any logic present at all, it would have told me one couldn't consume something that does not exist. It was not until Nick's death that I considered how extreme sadness overtakes a person.

Therapy sessions took place in our church's meditation room. We sat poised in high-back Victorian chairs with the Twelve Disciples looking down upon us from a painting on the wall. Rose-scented candles flickered on top of an antique table. I held on to my bitter remorse like a miser hoarding gold nuggets. What could happen if I bellowed out the hatred that polluted my heart? Could I lose my mind if I didn't? I had been taught to be reverent in the house of God and couldn't scream at Nick in front of Jesus and the Twelve. I had also learned to put on a smile and hide my darkest feelings. The purging would have to wait for an open, free, indestructible space.

Several quiet sessions went by. Alice introduced role-play and I edited my responses. Our last session left my stomach churning to the point of nausea. The children were safe with a baby-sitter, so instead of going home, I drove down country roads. Tears burned and blinded my eyes until I had to pull over.

A little white church surrounded by acres of corn sat baking under the hot sun and beckoned me closer. I felt like a thief in the night and feared the padded cell that onlookers might put me in if I allowed all of my anger to gush out.

The dusty softball field next to the church lured me over with one of the children's play balls tucked under my arm. Over and over I kicked the ball against the fence behind home plate. I screamed and kicked until exhaustion laid me down as my heart beat wildly against my chest. Now, when I grieve I turn on the shower and sob into the wet strands of flowing water.

Therapy can get intense, and it is up to the individual to set some boundaries. Stretch, work, and take a break. This is where journaling, doodling, and the identification of feelings can play a key part. Write, sit back, and discover what your heart wants to give. Identify the pain, the fear, and the guilt, and do something about it. Healing work is not for quitters, but a "quitter attitude" can be changed. Let love be your guide.

Remember to ask. People can't read your mind. Seek counseling from a professional therapist, a psychiatrist, a priest, or a physician. Join a support group such as Survivors of Suicide (S.O.S.), Attitudinal Healing, or Compassionate Friends. Include sculpting, drawing or painting (even if black is the only color you dip your brush into), journaling, physical activity, and conversation into your daily routine. Tell your stories, and ask for help.

If you feel horrible because you felt hatred or anger at your loved one, ask for love and forgiveness. Each person has the free will to ask or not to ask for the power of love. Take that first step toward help. Do not allow continuous hopeless thinking to overwhelm you. Prayer cleansed my brain of suicidal thoughts. A minister shared a personal story with me. He searched for a cure for depression for his wife. They met with out-of-state physicians skilled in working with depressed patients. She tried a number of antidepressants, but her depression prevailed. Once they even flew to Europe seeking a doctor with a miracle cure. Several years went by, and they stumbled upon something that eased her pain. Walking. Simple? I decided to try it because facing each day had become pure hell. Every morning I woke up and bundled our little Lauren in her stroller and walked around and around our neighborhood. My goal was to think of a positive thought. I headed for home when one seeped in and soothed my soul. Many weeks later the suicidal thoughts just disappeared. I continued to circle the neighborhood, but now on a new ten speed complete with child carrier on the back for Lauren. Guilt was fading. One Sunday on the way home from church Ross said, "My teacher told us to write about someone who we needed to forgive. I knew it was daddy, but I couldn't put down anything bad."

Journal

Write or draw about:

· **Write down your fear(s).**

· **Reflect upon your guilt.**

Journal

Write or draw about:

· **Forgiveness.**

Journal

Write or draw about:

· **What do you want to be forgiven for?**

Chapter 6

Self-Care

As a person isolates more and more, he loses the benefit of human feedback.

John Bradshaw

How does one receive support while in a frenzied state? Call 911... call God...? My husband did not ask.

"I don't need help... you do!" Had he ever known how to ask for what he truly wanted and needed? Was he delirious with clinical depression? Nick's state of mind at that crucial point in his life remains unknown. His energies as well as mine were spent supporting a façade to delay the pain of separation. Lives change when problems and needs are acknowledged. Change being the one guarantee in life.

Elisabeth Kubler-Ross in *Death and Dying* said, "Total acceptance, as in dying, is an existence without fear and despair." Ask for help and mark the beginning of your acceptance of your loved one's decision and death. One of the last things Nick said to me in our home came at the end of a heated battle of wills.

"I'm not afraid to die; I'm already living in hell." He was afraid to live. There were similar expressions listed in the stacks of suicide-prevention literature delivered after his death. Those signals however lay in a place called the past. There are four main questions to ask a person who hints that life isn't worth living: (1) Are you thinking about killing yourself? (2) How do you plan to do it? (3) When do you plan to do it? (4) Where do you plan to do it? Anyone who has a plan needs immediate help. Please call 911, a suicide crisis line, or a mental health provider and make a report.

Have you ever felt the urge to ask a question yet let it die on the tip of your tongue? Ask.

One Sunday in church, seven months after Nick's suicide, Reverend Avery announced the opening of the Center for Attitudinal Healing. My arms and legs tingled with a charge of electric energy. It was time for me to act on inspiration and intuition. How many times have you talked yourself out of doing something that you knew in your heart you were supposed to do? Fortunately, my survival instinct won and I attended the Attitudinal Healing orientation meeting in February 1988. Weekly meetings, self-discovery weekend retreats, and facilitator's training courses followed for three holy years.

Ross and Elizabeth joined the AH children's program. Lauren joined for one year when she was almost four. The children's facilitators were amazed at Lauren's ability to ask pertinent questions and redirect the group to the topic at hand. The children's program intertwined AH principles. The philosophy that love is greater than fear was at the center of action-packed discussions and games. These exercises helped the precious group of children weave through some of the loss, grief, and stressful issues invading their lives.

Each child copes with loss differently, and each child needs something extra safe to hold on to during the aftermath of suicide. The children colored, role-played, laughed, cried, and shared their stories. One night they met for a letting-go ceremony. They printed their good-bye balloons with messages that weighed heavily on their hearts and released them into the clouds. Each child watched the sky until the last balloon was out of sight. No one can explain the pain away or melt it with candy or kisses or promises. No one knows exactly how a son, a daughter, a brother, a sister, a cousin... will deal with severe loss. I prayed that the principles taught in AH would help Ross, Elizabeth, and Lauren with the ups and downs of life.

Dr. Gerald Jampolsky founded the first Center for Attitudinal Healing in Tiburon, California, in 1975. The twelve principles he outlined for AH became the breaths of fresh air I needed to begin my side of the suicide journey. Each adult meeting also focused on one of the twelve principles. Facilitators encouraged participants to focus on their feelings rather than on intellectual inventions. I have a special place in my heart for our director who called us on our tendencies toward secrecy. She mastered it all with love and I will always be grateful for her honesty and integrity.

Our diverse group of people included: an artist, two psychologists, several teachers, a voga instructor, two social workers, a nurse, several parents and a whimsical computer whiz. Each entered the group with one common goal: to achieve peace of mind. Some members had recently divorced, changed careers, suffered an illness, lost a loved one, or read the book *Love Is Letting Go of Fear* by Gerald Jampolsky and wanted to communicate on a healthier level.

During our second meeting a thin young woman spoke out, "He left me. I want to crawl in a deep, dark tunnel, fall asleep, and never get up." My stomach rolled with nausea. I wanted to scream, "No, don't do it; suicide hurts the people left behind." Another member shared, "I tried to kill myself with my three little children playing in the next room. I was so unhappy in my marriage. The Family Protective Services took my children away from me." My sick stomach tightened with anger, and I cried at the irony.

Had I been honest, I would have connected their fragilities with the night I looked around my house and spotted objects that I could have used to end my life. Love and courage led those brave women to share their stories. My courage was buried beneath fears of judgment and rejection. Many of us hide every flaw, every imperfection, and every inadequacy until we find that doing so isn't in our best interests.

The following Attitudinal Healing Principles filled my lungs with life, vigor, and a renewed sense of purpose:

1. The essence of our being is love.

2. Health is inner peace. Healing is letting go of fear.

3. Giving and receiving are the same.

4. We can let go of the past and of the future.

5. Now is the only time there is and each instant is for giving.

6. We can learn to love others and ourselves by forgiving rather than judging.

7. We can become love finders rather than faultfinders.

8. We can choose and direct ourselves to be peaceful inside, regardless of what is happening outside.

9. We are students and teachers to each other.

10. We can focus on the whole of life rather than the fragments.

11. Since love is eternal, death need not be viewed as fearful.

12. We can always perceive others as either extending love or giving a call for help.

I could write pages on each one, but instead, would like for you to explore these principles independent of my feelings and philosophies. Some of them may trigger anger, others tears. Whatever feelings arise, explore them, share them and love them just because they are a part of you.

Journal

Write or draw about:

· **Lightly scan the list of principles and allow yourself the privilege of exploring the one that speaks to you now. How do you feel?**

Journal

Write or draw about:

· **What does death look like right now?**

· **How would you like for it to look?**

Journal

Write or draw about:

· Is there a careless comment circling around in your mind? Write it down as you remember it.

· How did it feel upon hearing those words?

Journal

Write or draw about:

· **How have you questioned yourself?**

· **Has suicide ever tried to pull you over to its side?**

Chapter 7

Camping Out in Hell's Graveyard

Until we challenge the reality of our ego, we will continue to go through life more concerned with getting than giving, feeling guilty, separate, and afraid. We will make condemning judgments, blaming others and ourselves.

**With the ego as our guide,
guilt and fear will rule our lives.**

Gerald Jampolsky, M.D.

Denial, anger, and bargaining spun me around in circles for months. Late one night I heard the tinkling of car keys outside our house. Panic stricken, I expected Nick to unlock the front door and walk right in. "Sorry, I'm late. I needed time to think, to clear my head." I shook and waited for him to appear. I was furious that he could show up, unannounced after pulling us through hell's flames. Was I losing my mind? Denial allowed me to bargain for the time I needed so that I could bury him once and for all.

The twilight visitor turned out to be one of his best friends, Allen, whom I had not seen since the funeral. I looked at him and wondered, "Does he blame me?" He answered with a story.

"Nick always said if things ever got too bad... a terminal illness, if you ever left him... he'd kill himself." No wonder his nerves were a wreck. The option of suicide was in the back of Nick's mind since before we had met. Health, economics, our fragile relationship were the pillars that if they crumbled he would go down with them. His friend disclosed that he had talked Nick out of suicide years earlier following a break up with his high school sweetheart. We shared some Harley Davidson tales and mourned the waste of a talented man.

"Why didn't he call me this time?" Allen asked on his way out. Why didn't he call me? I thought. Why, why, why? But, all I could say was, he didn't want you to stop him.

Do you remember any outbursts prior to the suicide? Was there a calm before the storm smashed through your life?

Nick threatened, "You'll be so sorry!" and I scowled back indignantly. Hindsight revealed red flags bleeding with skulls and crossbones. Why couldn't I see them in his fisted hands? Empty your heart and soul of the memories that bind you. Discover your special way to release them. Digging up painful memories will not be as bad as hiding them inside.

My brain throbbed with our last telephone conversation. We'll find a way to lead separate lives, I told him.

"It will be hard," he confided. We hung up confused and unsettled. A sudden death leaves no good-byes. Loved ones can't hold hands around the dying person's bed and bid farewell respectfully. Instead, the family is bombarded with a load of unfinished business. Battering regrets turned into deep clinical depression as I obsessively tried to change our last conversation.

One cannot blanket suffering. We wake up shivering and know we must face the icy truth. Identify the pain. Is it guilt or anger or depression? Blow up the bop bag if you need to, and pounce on it until the pain leaks out. The suicide is not your mistake to cover. Rest, rejuvenate and ask, what positive action can I take now? Design your destiny with questions that focus on moving forward, through the pain. Saying good-bye to your loved one is not forgetting about him or her. If we get stuck bargaining, reenacting a favorable or unfavorable scene, ruminating real or unreal transgressions then we will never wave, turn, and go on. Be aware that the ultimate bargain is the vow to never discuss the suicide.

Were you handed a Bible locked in a cedar box? Mine smelled like an old forest as my eyes stumbled over the embossed gold script, In Loving Memory. Those words carried me back to the curb in front of our house. I didn't feel loving, and he didn't feel loved. It took months before I could open that Holy Book. I was terrified that every line would substantiate the verse... to love thy neighbor as thyself. The work at hand involved getting beyond the wish that I had loved him more and scrutinized him less.

Guilt traps us in the past. Did you talk to your loved one at the service? Unworthiness bound my hands to my side unable to touch his casket. How could I stand by a dead man who sacrificed himself on the words "till death do us part?" Guilt twisted my intestines into knots. Thirteen years of our lives were stuffed into scrapbooks; reminders of happier days that fueled more guilt. Picture after picture; the bits and pieces of our youth now overflowed our bedroom trash basket. Write down your wretched thoughts and misunderstandings before you rip up your valuables.

One of my favorite vacation snapshots of Nick was taken in St. Augustine, Florida. He sat under a dreamy palm tree in cut-off blue jeans with an ice cream sandwich in one hand and a long-necked Stroh's beer in the other. We experienced the world through the eyes of needy children and ignorance is not bliss. The emotional roller coaster had squealed through family holidays, adventures across different states and ended on individual sides of Nick's suicide. I didn't want to revisit memories of the tears he held back when Ross, Elizabeth, and Lauren were cradled in his arms for the very first time.

If you have the urge to tear, shred, rip... and can't find a pen, there's always a phone book or bag of newspapers lying around somewhere. Snatch one up. Rip, pull, and tear your heartache out. Burn the pile of trash then scrub your hands of the slick black residual darkness. Let your heart settle back down inside the warmth of your chest.

Are you running away or taking a break? Our society has an antidote for every pain. Don't struggle, we are told. Take an aspirin, a tranquilizer, drink a beer, and cover your tear-streaked face.

"Just don't think about it, you can't move back father time," my friend said. Ross wanted to build a time machine and travel back before the suicide and help his dad get well. How does one stop hopeless thinking? We are living, breathing, thinking organisms and have been taught to analyze. There was a time when the words, "I'm never going to get over this," were chiseled into my brain. Get rid of that nasty word never!

Steven Levine offers support in his book, *Guided Meditations, Explorations and Healings*, which helps us get beyond the excuses and open up to healing. He states that finishing business means that I open my heart to you, that whatever blocks my heart with resentment or fear, whatever I still want from you is let go of and I just send love. I open to you as you are, not as I wish you to be or as I wish me to be. I no longer look to be forgiven or to show others how unfair they were. Stop holding back love and forgiveness and you will heal... and, those around you will be helped along the way as well.

There are creative ways to sidestep guilt. Zip here, there and run circles around yourself until you are impelled to nothing but obligatory activities. Work day and night until your appointment book bulges with colorful distractions, until you are too tired to tell someone dear that you need to talk. We grieve for ourselves. Let your broken heart gape open. There is a place just beyond where relief awaits you. Walk through the rain shower. Moan like a mother giving birth, howl like a lone wolf.

Is responsibility the fourth "r" to be listed along with reading, writing, and arithmetic? Is it the missing link that eludes us most of the time? Rather than searching for guilt, let us right the so-called wrongs in our world and move forward. Survivors are thrivers in the rough.

Susan Trout stated that in the search for wholeness there is no one-way. There is only your way. On your side of suicide, feelings will revisit you. A familiar melody may float over the gate from your neighbor's stereo and remind you of a time that you and your loved one shared. Express the feelings that hang suspended inside of you and let them fly.

What happens when we do not take the time to feel? Lucas and Seiden, in *Silent Grief* share that survivors may suffer from a multitude of medical problems such as alcoholism, drug addiction, psychosomatic symptoms, headaches, sinus problems, stomach ailments, and heart attacks.

Physical and mental illness become a way of identifying with or punishing oneself for a loved one's suicide. If a survivor is angry enough, he or she may consider suicide as a justifiable punishment. Stop those thoughts from growing. Thoughts of killing myself darted crazily in and out of my mind. Self-sabotage plotted its deadly course until I asked God to take those lethal injections away from me. Answers flowed: sing, cry, play racquetball... write... doodle. Take one step, then another.

Talk to your family members and let them cry. Tears often show up out of sequence. Elizabeth had wanted to live with her daddy if we divorced. Little girls look up to their fathers to lead them, love them, and cherish them. Devastated, she did not shed one tear in public.

Stunned, she asked, "Killed himself... why?"

Weeks later a pair of kittens pitter-pattered into our lives, adding two joyful hearts to four shattered ones. The playful little fur balls also scratched furniture, shredded drapes, stained the carpets, and racked my frayed nerves. I gathered the children together and told them the kittens were just too much trouble right now. Elizabeth cried and cried and cried. The loss of anything else was inconceivable. We made their new bed in Nick's garage beneath the workbench.

Journal

Write or draw about:

· **Share the story inside of you that is aching to be told.**

Chapter 8

Dreams

To move closer to love, we must sometimes move away from it. At times it is only by distancing ourselves, temporarily, from a seemingly hopeless situation that we can begin to engage in the acts necessary for regeneration.

Leo Buscaglia

Quiet nights cradle all kinds of dreams. Every night I went to bed peering into a ghost of my late husband's angry eyes. He stared at me until I fell asleep. His image appeared in the same place each morning at 3 o'clock. Night after night, dreams reinforced the guilt that riddled my mind. In one dream I sat in a courtroom and faced the judge while the verdict guilty or not guilty was undecided. Who had killed my husband?

Someone I didn't recognize was being cross-examined, and all of a sudden I jumped up and screamed, "I did it. I killed him." Case closed. I woke up in a sick, scared sweat. It's over, and I am guilty. I believed it and didn't tell a soul about the dream for several years. I continued to incarcerate myself with blame. What kind of a horrible person becomes a widow from the suicide of a sad, angry, talented man? Suicide was no dream. It was an irreversible nightmare that haunted me throughout the first four stages of bereavement.

Guilt prevailed until I scratched the first few chapters of this book down in my journal. I relived the dream, felt tension deep inside my belly, and scribbled the scene, fast, before fear stopped my pen. I needed to tell someone and get the enormous weight off of my chest. The courtroom event exploded before me like fireworks on the Fourth of July. This time I pounded the gavel and imprisoned myself behind the bars of guilt. Now I call it Post-Traumatic Stress Disorder (PTSD).

"God, help me," I asked, and climbed out of bed and shuffled into the living room. The bookshelf Nick had crafted for me pulled me over and presented me with our memorial Bible. I read in Job 3:25, "For what I fear comes upon me, and what I dread befalls me." Our thoughts attract things. We often wonder why a good person suffers. The Bible revealed that Job lived in a constant state of fear. He spent his life worrying about the feasts and fortunes he would surely lose. Fear attracts negativity. I was afraid

45

I had sinned against Nick, and thus, tucked myself in each night looking into his glaring eyes. In Job 1: 6-12, Satan complained that the Lord had blessed the work of Job, and he wanted to place a curse in his hands. The Lord said unto Satan, "Behold, all that he hath is in thy power; only upon himself put not forth thine hand." Only Job could take away Job's blessing. Job's fearful thoughts of losing everything eventually came true for him.

Fearful thoughts keep us glued to the words that all survivors ask at some time or another, Why me? Why have I failed? Ask instead show me how to reach peace of mind. Show me how to forgive myself. Show me Your Love.

Hours of middle-of-the-night reading later I blinked and Nick's pasty white image slipped away forever. My life would rebuild according to the standards, values, talents, and needs which stirred inside of me. The sick, scared sweat evaporated and the constant thoughts of, "I killed him," dried up. The freedom to heal emerged. Dreams don't lie, of course, but they dutifully portray our innermost fears. Choose to grow and love and live. Healing is an option, life a privilege, and guilt is the wall that blocks them both.

Months after the courtroom verdict had been filed away another dream materialized starring Nick in the driver's seat of a yellow Volkswagen bug and two dear buddies in the back. The dream played out like an old-time movie where actors sit close up in a parked car and the highway scene races on behind. Inside the bright yellow bubble, the three men talked and laughed. Nick turned his head toward me, smiled broadly, and showed his perfect white teeth.

He looked into my eyes and waved, "I am happier here. It was just too hard to change." He was glowing with a joy I hadn't seen in years. My heart pulsed with love for him. The dream was a one-time showing that rescued me from phobic scenarios of him burning in the pits of hell. He was living life on a different level now and was not alone. How could I love him more now than ever before?

Anthony Robbins lectures to people about their motivations. He teaches that we are motivated by the desire for pleasure or the desire to avoid pain. Suicidal individuals are focused on the desire to avoid pain and may not be able to consider anyone else's feelings at all. They project all of their pain into their futures. They say, "I can't face it," and choose to avoid it altogether. Survivor pain is often equal to or greater than the pain experienced by those who end their lives. No judgment intended here. People are unique and possess varying degrees of stamina. There is hope after the pain.

Native American shamans mentored to their young apprentices. They honored pain and said to touch it, breathe it, and dive right into it. They encouraged the village healers and the sick alike to feel the intensity and the heat of the pain and swim through to the soft warm sand on the other side. We can have peace when we travel through our grief.

Journal

Write or draw about:

· **Empty your guilty conscience.**

· **What does your guiltless life look like?**

Journal

Write or draw about:

· **Have you dreamed of your loved one? Write down your dreams. There is a message in each one.**

Journal

Chapter 9

Rituals

I have always thought of Christmastime as a good time; a kind, forgiving, generous, pleasant time; a time when men and women open their hearts freely; and so I say "God bless Christmas."

Emily Dickenson

December 1987. The first Christmas without Nick was sliding in fast. I didn't feel. We didn't feel. What was there to celebrate? Elizabeth, Ross, Lauren, and I huddled around our kitchen table early one morning before the sun splashed the walls with pink, orange and purple. Just days before, hadn't we carved pumpkins? A few short months ago Nick shared oatmeal with his kids. He always buttered it like bread. He stirred it slowly while it melted and winked across the table at his kids who watched, stirred and settled into a new day with their daddy close-by. His Christmas gift had to be the first.

We spread the table with newspapers, scissors, pinecones, floral wire and a large metal circle. Each child held out a branch thick with the scent of an evergreen wood. We twisted the wire around and around, added pinecones and talked about the things their daddy liked to do. We talked about the toys he made for them and remembered his love and spirit for life. Those times were buried until now.

The children ventured out into the house and brought back little treasures from their toy boxes and dresser drawers. We twisted each one onto the wreath, tightly, as though it would somehow last forever. The never-ending circle of love was covered with family mementos. Ross brought a tiny baseball glove and a miniature Harley Davidson. Elizabeth brought a pearl white heart and a silver cross from her jewelry box. We tied the wreath with a huge red satin ribbon my grandma gave me years before.   Lauren, now two, left the room disinterested with the project or so we thought! Her soft blue eyes twinkled as she returned, opened her precious hopeful hand, and offered up a white angel with golden painted wings. The Christmas tree with the new bare spot seemed to stand proud, knowing the angel had a higher purpose now. We bound it to the wreath and were done.

A few days later we drove to the cemetery, placed the wreath on Nick's grave, and said our prayers. We laughed and cried on the way home as we talked about the good times we spent with Daddy. Each time we visited, I marked the changes in us as well as the changes in our gift. The wreath withstood the midwest winter winds.

April melted the earth's frozen crust and daffodils popped brightly through the drab terrain. We decided to cut the first bouquet for Nick and traveled the road to the cemetery again. The children ran to the grave and slid to a stop. The lawn attendant had disposed of their daddy's wreath! Nestled between the earth and the fresh green grass was the little white angel with the golden wings. We thought about picking it up and bringing it home. Ross, Elizabeth, and Lauren were happy it survived and decided to leave it in its new place to watch over their daddy. Maybe, it is still there maybe not. Somehow each one of us realized we couldn't bring the wreath back; we couldn't bring Nick back; and we couldn't stay there sinking in the soft, wet earth.

Journal

Write or draw about:

· **Do you have a closing ceremony in mind?**

Journal

Chapter 10

Angry Again?

You're never upset for the reason you think.

Dr. Gerald Jampolsky

My purpose in writing this book is to create a sacred space for you to reflect upon your side of suicide with the one side I am most familiar. I couldn't possibly live inside of our children's minds, hearts, and souls and share their feelings about suicide. Their truths would be lost; their sides obscured with my translation.

Loved ones will look to you for guidance, not answers. They intuitively know their answers are within. Inside I wanted to help our children reach peace. Outside I covered up pent up anger and pain. Children have a direct connection to our hearts, regardless of what we paint on our faces. Your family needs to watch you go through the grieving process and be included in it.

Days were dull and hopeless until I admitted my anger toward Nick. It took years to vent the anger I had silently packed away. Ross and I broke his Little League Slugger in half seven years after Nick died. We took turns slamming a sawed off tree stump. Each swing splintered bitterness, self-hatred, and the pain of abandonment into small, manageable slivers. I mourned the safe, secure, happy-go-lucky childhood for which Ross, Elizabeth, and Lauren were robbed. Tears once more opened the door to a future of love and peace and adventure.

"Parental suicide is one of the worst kinds of child abuse," my therapist said, and I went red. Why had I lifted Nick's name out of the dripping sludge only to give the children a false sense of their own anger? No more. We were mad and this time no words would be altered or edited out of our expressions.

He had backed everyone up against the wall of life, love, and dreams when he said, "Watch me. You'll be sorry you didn't give me what I demanded, sorry you didn't listen to my constant complaints of never getting, getting, getting enough. You'll be sorry you put yourselves first."

Linda, a dear friend shared that her father died when she was five. "It is like coming home and everything's gone. You search in all of the rooms for something familiar to touch, but the house is empty." Elizabeth had asked to live with Nick after our divorce. She wanted and needed more of his attention. She too was five when her daddy died and covered up the pain that surrounded her loss. Unfortunately, she didn't join me late at night in the black backyard when I was smashing kick balls, weeding the garden, and painting swing sets. Elizabeth, Lauren and Ross saw me showered and refreshed in the mornings, again robbed of the most important phase of bereavement. Anger.

What was I afraid of? Would it kill me? Could their unresolved anger kill them? Would their anger blame me? Years ago I was afraid to talk about the threats that he needled under my skin, and the careless message, "I don't need you!" that I shot back at him. The fear of losing our children's trust towered over the hundreds of little daily opportunities to discuss their daddy's death and what it meant to them.

Nick tossed his tormented heart and mind into the innocent palms of our children. He left three precious souls to clean up the consequences of his decision to die. He gave up, and yes, it was OK to be angry and show it! Finally surviving, we were on our way toward thriving.

Inner conflicts are as damaging to the body and soul as external ones. *Love, Medicine and Miracles* by Dr. Bernie Siegel states, "When patients resolve conflicts they find new energy to heal. If we could do this with all of our patients we would probably increase the number of self-induced cures dramatically." Nick must not have known how much his children were going to miss him, how the legacy of his death would affect them, how much they wanted to grow up with him. He just didn't know at the time.

Journal

Write or draw about:

· **There is no one to blame.**

Journal

Write or draw about:

· **How will you honor your anger?**

Journal

Write or draw about:

· **What does freedom from guilt look and feel like to you?**

Chapter 11

Acceptance

Out of every crisis comes the choice to be reborn, to reconceive ourselves as individuals, to choose the kind of change that will help us to grow and fulfill ourselves more completely.

Nena O'Neill

Suicide leaves a family in a state of confusion that takes months and often years to unravel. A tornado of guilt, anger and despair ripped through your home and left layers of debris. Scrape through the layers of "if only" and take responsibility for complete, thriving recovery.

Our lives had reached out for each other years before. I loved excitement and someone to care for and control. Nick loved adventure and someone to protect and manipulate. We were equally matched and equally responsible for the relationship that we created. The sickness doesn't stop just because one half of the pair is no longer alive. The vicious cycle continues until we stop it. We couldn't sprinkle magic powder on Nick's decayed limbs, renew marriage vows, sit through hours of couple's counseling and start all over. I could however, spread love over every curve, cell and memory of him and trust in the power of survival.

The fact remained that Nick's battle was over and letting go of him was the only solution. I peeled my fingers back one-by-one from the sick need to control life and started to heal from the inside out. The random, phobic thoughts, "I've lost a part of myself and I will never be the same," finally began to fade. The truth is, life would be different.

Your loved one had reasons which made life too complicated to deal with. The saddest mistake would be to blame. Richard Nelson and Judith Galas, in *The Power To Prevent Suicide*, wrote that suicidal people live in the present and can't think about time curing all ills. They are plagued with ambivalence and want to live and die at the same time. Suicidal individuals believe that they must live with their painful feelings and terrible problems or must die to escape them. Since options are limited, they want to get it over with quickly and are unable to consider anyone else's feelings. Our deceased loved ones were locked into a self-destructive state of mind.

Help yourself! Your loved one would want you to move forward. Many years of growth and change have gone by since Nick's suicide. Ross, Elizabeth, and Lauren have graduated high school and continue to move on with their lives. Grandparents have aged, loved, and blessed us.

My father's youth was trapped inside a stiff hardened shell called Parkinson's Disease for ten years before he died in 1998. He used to win the history trivia games on Friday afternoons and shared his last two years in a nursing home with Hershel. Hershel was 96 years old and had lost his wife of seventy-five years.

Hershel confided, "I just can't shake the blues. I can get around easy enough. Your dad falls a lot. Most people around here can't go to the bathroom alone. I know why some people take their lives." Gentle, shrewd, intuitive? Warm, honest tears washed our eyes.

Still guilty? Guilt has but one advantage, and that is to point to the need to self-correct. Letting go of guilt opens up opportunities to give and to receive love.

It was hard for me to admit to myself that I was equally at fault for creating a marriage based on power struggles, manipulation, and control. It was harder to admit this flaw in public. What would I gain from keeping my angry outbursts, self-pity, and controlling behaviors a secret? Well, I could stay sick and remain a victim attached to the past forever. Fortunately, it no longer added up.

Mourning the loss of a loved one is moving forward into unknown territory and freedom. Move with grace! No one is guilty. There are people dying to live and just as many waiting to die. People seek miracle medicines and psychotherapy to add quality to their lives while others do not believe a quality life is possible and turn from their cures. Some dear ones cannot wait for their human existence to end and recklessly die by their own hands. We make our decisions based on our unique backgrounds, experience, and knowledge. Some unsolved mysteries are best left unsolved.

"What can I do with the list of possible reasons which pushed my loved one over the edge?" This is different than searching for why. Why did he or she do it? Accept that you may never know why, and acknowledge that something private can remain private. Honor the unknown. We don't have to know why.

One of the hardest practices in our culture is writing a letter of apology, good-bye, or request for a special favor. The burden that you carry requires the incorporation of all three and perhaps more. Anne Brener in her book, *Mourning & Mitzvah* suggests writing a letter to your deceased loved one.

The journal entries in *One Side of Suicide* may also be used to help you outline your letter. The following exercise has the potential to empty your mind, body, and soul of unfinished business so that you can reclaim your rights to a life of freedom, abundance, peace and joy.

As suggested by Anne Brener take the time and fill out a similar questionnaire below.

Date

Dear

1. It has been   since your death.

2. When they told me you were dead ...

3. During your funeral, I felt...

4. I still hear these words from you inside of my head...

5. When I want to be with you I feel...

6. Something I remember when I think of you is...

7. The last thing I remember that you said to me was...

8. Memories of you make me feel...

9. Something that I didn't tell you when you were alive is...

10. Your death was so sudden. I hadn't expected...

11. After I found you (found out that you died), I...

12. If you were alive today, I...

13. Something I feel guilty about is...

14. The hardest thing for me to do is...

15. The hardest thing for me to accept is...

16. The thing I fear the most is...

17. One thing that I am still angry about is...

18. I'd like you to know this about who I am now...

19. Something I talked about with your family/friends is...

20. In losing you, I feel that I have lost...

21. I wish you could be here to help me with...

22. I would like you to forgive me about...

23. Something(s) that I have experienced since your death...

24. I would also like to ask you...

25. What I always wanted to hear you say was...

26. You didn't understand that...

27. What I would like to know about you is...

28. I wish you could have understood...

29. What I would like for you to know about me is...

30. The thing I resent the most is...

31. I am most grateful for...

32. What I have learned about you since your death is...

33. The thing I feel most guilty about when thinking about you is...

34. What I don't miss about you is...

35. What I miss the most is...

36. A favorite story I like to tell about you is...

37. The grief I will endure about you is...

38. Something that I will do differently in my life because of what you did in yours is...

39. Despite the things that separate us, the things we share are...

40. My dearest hope for you now is that you...

Signed,

Journal

Write or draw about:

· **How does it feel to have written a letter to your loved one?**

Journal

Write or draw about:

· What message would you like to leave your loved ones?

· On parting, what would you like for them to know about you?

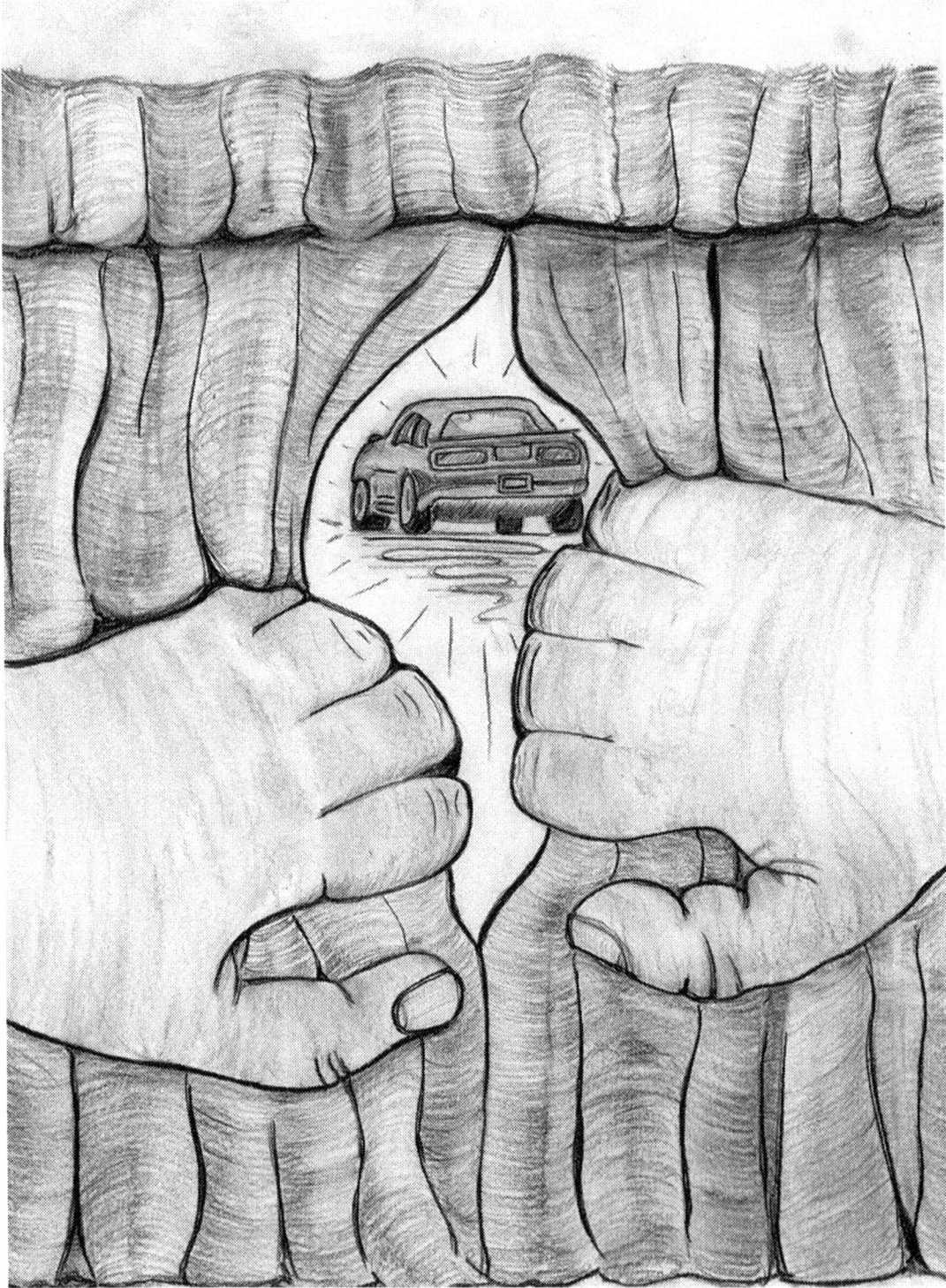

Chapter 12

Forgiveness

There is no medicine like hope, no tonic more powerful than the belief that every trauma has a solution. For those who believe, hope does, indeed, spring eternal.

Leo Buscaglia

Forgiveness always brings a new dimension to life; hope. Every trauma holds its solution in the middle of its pain. Forgiveness nurtured my walk and guiltlessness cleared a pathway to hope. I had experienced self-hatred and hatred of Nick. The quickest way to experience hell is to harbor hate. I watched my family bow their heads as they followed my footsteps through the iron gates of guilt. The words, "It's not your fault," didn't mean anything to children who listened for hidden messages between the lines, "I wish I could have loved Daddy more. I wish I hadn't complained so much. I wish he had known I loved him too."

You can't fool children. If you are feeling guilty say so. Work on dissolving it, together, if possible. The invisible shackles of guilt chained us to his responsibility more times than I would like to remember. We danced around conversations that trudged too close to our secret. We wore fake smiles in our attempts to forgive and forget. My husband's deceased. The children's father passed away. My lips melted together like glue and suicide stuck on the back of my tongue.

The first time I shared my whole story with a new friend and colleague I wondered, "Will she think I'm crazy?" Fifteen years later we are still friends, life-long buddies brought together through honesty, courage and love.

I made a million mistakes, and I hope I will make a million more. Mistakes have taken on a new meaning. They represent individual motivations for trying, changing, and doing things a little differently; a bit more lovingly, honestly. I had wasted precious energy feeling sorry for myself and for my children. Forgiveness warmed my soul, and connected me to everything beautiful. The trees, flowers, and landscape took on a reverence. Appreciation filled my heart and our children echoed the rhythm and lightened up their steps too. I pray they rinse themselves free of every single sorrow the suicide caused them. I am forever grateful for their love and incredible compassion. Forgive and your life will change for the better. Everyday miracles will appear out of the fog.

Forgiveness was the key I turned to open the door to a vibrant new life. I thank God every day for Ross, Elizabeth, Lauren, my family, dear friendships, the Center for Attitudinal Healing, a college graduation, a spiritual center, a new town, a new marriage and a precious baby girl.

Our lives will always be different because Nick was with us. Gratefully his spirit for joy continues on in us and for us. Fear still comes and goes as new situations arise. Our family mission now is to look fear and doubt in the eye, stand strong on a foundation of truth, and take whatever action is called for.

Yes, there are other times swirled with the challenges of parenthood, self-assertiveness, and procrastination. I have overprotected, under protected, and bored my children to tears with lectures on how to avoid some of the major pitfalls of life. If fear cripples you in the day or in the night, remember to ask for guidance, forgiveness, and the strength to move the dark mountains. Trust they will fade and disappear into the past and the power of love and hope will light up every cell in your body.

Judith Viorst, in *Necessary Losses* describes parenting dreams that arise in new parents as the dreams of keeping babies safe from harm. Even the loftiest schemes for our children's happiness and well being may insult their integrity. Teach them to love, forgive, and ask for help and they will succeed in life.

Where was Nick's help? People kept showing up to help me. A friend of Nick's told me he had stopped by to see Nick a week before his death and found no car in sight and all of the drapes pulled. He knocked at the door anyway but left it unanswered. Just as he started up his car, he noticed a brush of movement in the drapes, a slight opening that hadn't been there a moment before. He deduced Nick did not want to be bothered and drove away. His friend would have been greeted curbside on prior occasions; clinical, untreated, depression. Forgive situations no one has any control over.

Life guarantees change. Dr. Gerald Jampolsky steers people toward a guilt free life by asking them to imagine what it would be like to wake up with no worries or anxieties, fears, guilt or past grievances, and no doubts or uncertainties about the future. Guilt or forgiveness, which is it going to be?

Journal

Write or draw about:

· **We've hid, asked, cried, and prayed. Is there a fear tucked away that you are ready to express?**

Journal

Write or draw about:

· **Is there something or someone who you took for granted?**

Journal

Write or draw about:

· **How do you feel when you let go of guilt?**

$\mathcal{J}ournal$

Write or draw about:

· **What would you have wanted your loved one to do with his or her desperation?**

Journal

Write or draw about:

· **What comforts you?**

· **What helps you feel secure?**

Chapter 13

The Choice to Thrive

The more joy there can be in the marriage between dead and living, the better. I have discovered, passionate grief does not link us with the dead but cuts us off from them.

C.S. Lewis

We cannot change the past, yet we can live in it if we choose. We can travel to a point in time and remain there for years. We can also travel to that same point, feel it, express it, learn from it, and lastly, we can let it go. We can review a million little scenes and gently close the curtain after each one, knowing the curtain may, rise again. The players will perform until they tire of the script. When the final act is played out, allow yourself to celebrate.

I like to remember my husband in his workshop early in the morning, late into the night, whistling like no one else could. Nick's workbench had a pile of tools on one side and Ross, wearing purple Adidas swim trunks and brown cowboy boots on the other.

"Give me a quarter-inch socket, Rosso," and thoughtfully the tool was placed in his daddy's open palm. The love they passed from hand to hand remains forever blessed. Faith the size of a mustard seed can move mountains and a handful of love can supply a soul for a lifetime.

Nick's life was not meaningless because he died by suicide. Thank your loved one for being in your life. Honor your loved one too. You are not supporting the way he or she left or judging the rightness or wrongness of the death. You are, however, giving credit to the magnificence present in the life he or she lived.

Nick was solid as a rock when his children were in need. Elizabeth spent a week in the hospital after she and her bicycle collided with a car. He begged time off work and cradled her into the pediatric unit's little red wagon. Father and daughter rolled by a lot of open doors that week thankful that he would be bringing her home.

Allow the following words from the Unity Truth Center to energize you during this transition from acceptance to thriving:

I am a perfect expression of Love.

The Love within me comforts me, protects me, and gives me great joy to live my life.
I am safe in the midst of incredible change.

Repeat them over and over until you feel safe. Crowd out words of pessimism, doubt, fear, and hatred. Speak words that feed your soul. Remember, change takes courage and life is change.

I've heard the following message in so many circles, from so many dear people that I must repeat it here for you:

It would be well for all of us, whether we've been told we had a terminal illness or not, to live each day as if it were the very last one we had. If we did, we'd spend our very precious time doing only what was essential, meaningful, and joyful. We'd never take anyone or anything for granted and quickly take care of any unfinished business.

So much has happened since I started this book. College gently pulled me through classes, textbooks, and goals. Yes, I ran from my pain in the only acceptable way that I could, in the name of education. I loved every single minute of it and regret not a one. I put on my graduation gown and scanned the rows of families. My husband, Paul, Ross, Elizabeth, Lauren, and our new baby girl, Ali smiled from their seats in Assembly Hall. Together we celebrated moving onward and upward. This time tears marked joy, happiness, and awe. Life can be rebuilt. Let yourself soar. Listen to your inner stirrings for future missions and thrive.

Nick will touch us forever, as your loved one will touch you. Stand up, accept, and receive your precious gift of life now. Know that you are worthy of such a special gift. Visualize your loved one in acceptance of the same. Trust in the power, feelings, knowledge, and support that pulsate through your entire being every second of every day. Hold your loved one in your heart like an eternal friend, in a part of your soul that will always live. Let the mysterious, unyielding scariness of death dissolve and open up your life for transformative bliss.

There are no apologies needed for the number of years chewed up in search of peace. Join my celebration, hold hands, and grasp in the delight. The grief that you experience, the feelings you accept and express can evolve into an abundance of healing love. This type of love is all that is real on earth and will nourish your thriving spirit.

A number of Nature's appointed angels have carried me throughout the writing of these memories. I have been blessed with a no-strings-attached love for just being me and am so grateful for each and everyone who listened and did not judge me, who listened, judged, but did not condemn, who loved me and who still do. This life has given me an unwavering belief in the strength and spirit within each human being. I invite you to join me in understanding that today begins the rest of your life. Allow freedom to flow into your soul and celebrate your life, your love, and your wholeness.

Journal

Write or draw about:

· **What ways do you accept yourself now?**

· **How can you use self-acceptance in your everyday life?**

· **What ways do you accept your loved one?**

EPILOGUE

I worked on an adolescent psychiatric unit for six years as the educational specialist. The position translated into "teacher of math, English, writing, and career development." My daily routine entailed caring for patients who were stressed out and hard pressed for ideas to carry them over life's bumpy, sometimes hazardous, roads. Basically, the ticket onto the locked unit was suicidal ideation or attempt. Patients stared at their assignments with varying degrees of attitude; some felt hopeless, others competent yet unmotivated, and others angry. A few called the Emergency Room doctors, "bastards" for the charcoal drink that made them puke.

Our nurse knocked on the classroom door and called a precious teenager out of my class more times than I want to remember to check bandaged wrists.
"I wanted to die. There is nothing left for me to live for and you can't make me do anything in here!" The nurse peeled off the gauze, "OK, they're ready to come out," and clipped the tiny black stitches that walked across the thin, pale wrists. The young beauty had slit them in a cry for help. It was a last resort to stop the overwhelming pain.

What was I doing sowing algebra seeds in minds that calculated zeros in self-worthiness? I planted them with hope and love and put the math away just before their eyes glazed over. We moved on to hands on projects related to hobbies, career development, travel and literature. We played games together, listed goals and outlined action plans. The teens taught me more about hypocrisy, social injustice, and unresolved grief than I could have ever dreamed to teach them. Their scars scabbed over, tears dried up, a smile or two returned to their faces and they began to share their unique stories.

"I didn't really want to kill myself. I was so mad, so sad; I hated myself." I never told them, "I know, dear one, my husband was mad, sad, too. The day I filed for divorce he snuffed his life out with carbon monoxide poisoning." Instead, I simply shared, "I've lost a very dear friend to suicide. Stay with us. We each have a reason to be here." Love silently poured out of my heart to them and Nick.

I thrive because I've been touched more than once by an angel who brought me out of myself, out of depression and self-pity, and loved me into pursuing the work I am meant to do. You will too. We impact our families and our communities and thrive through the appreciation of life; a life that once felt deep sadness. Our life experience formulates our personal viewpoints. We value joy and happiness because we have known their opposites. Thriving is blessing both ends of your experience and everything in between. This is your time to shine in the glory of being a feeling, pulsing, wise child of the Universe. Excel, it is your nature! Love yourself for staying alive and making the commitment to heal. Ask for your mission and feel your love for life grow and blossom. Ask what you are to do next and how you are to thrive. Your answers will show up. I promise.

The day I asked for my mission, an image of one of my adolescent psychiatric patients holding his classroom assignment unfolded in front of my eyes. Matt, who had pointed a gun to his head two weeks earlier was seventeen, hooked on cocaine, a high school dropout. He prefaced most of his comments with, "You see, I'm a little slow. What did you say I was supposed to do?"

Matt introduced his project to our little class of ten with, "Here's my ghetto map." He pointed to his carefully designed travel brochure that opened up into thirds showing a beautiful sketch of the Congo River. He marked his destination points with brightly colored markers, red for the river, blue for the cities, and orange for the mountains. Matt educated us on the exciting places he had chosen to research.

"You see, I'm an out-of-doors type of person. That's why I chose the Congo River. I figure you can't get much more out-of-doors than that." In the end we clapped in gratitude for his creativity and investment.

My mission: Be a teacher for life, a student for life, and a thriving, surviving explorer of life.

Journal

Appendix A

12 Principles of Attitudinal Healing

1. The essence of our being is love.

2. Health is inner peace. Healing is letting go of fear.

3. Giving and receiving are the same.

4. We can let go of the past and of the future.

5. Now is the only time there is and each instant is for giving.

6. We can learn to love others and ourselves by forgiving rather than judging.

7. We can become love finders rather than faultfinders.

8. We can choose and direct ourselves to be peaceful inside, regardless of what is happening outside.

9. We are students and teachers to each other.

10. We can focus on the whole of life rather than the fragments.

11. Since love is eternal, death need not be viewed as fearful.

12. We can always perceive others as either extending love or giving a call for help.

Appendix B

Suggested Reading List for Adults

Arthur, Jonathan (2002). **The angel and the dragon: a father's search for answers to his son's mental illness and suicide.** Health Communications. Deerfield Beach, FL

Baugher, Bob. Ph.D., and Jack Jordan, Ph.D. (2002). **After suicide loss: coping with your grief**. Available through AFSP.

Biskup, Michael & Wekesser, Carol (1992). **Suicide: opposing viewpoints.** Greenhaven Press. San Diego.

Carlson, Trudy (2000). **Suicide survivor's handbook-expanded edition.** Benline Press.

DiGiulio, Robert (1989). **Beyond widowhood: from bereavement to emergence and hope.** Free Press, New York.

Dunne, Edward, McIntosh, John and Dunne-Maxim, Karen (Eds.) (1987). **Suicide and its aftermath: understanding and counseling the survivors.** W.W. Norton and Company.

Grollman, Earl (1995). **Bereaved children and teens: a support guide for parents and professionals.** Beacon Press. Boston.

Jamison, Kay and Knopf, Alfred (1995). **An unquiet mind: a memoir of moods and madness.** New York.

Jamison, Kay (1999). **Night falls fast: understanding suicide.** Knopf. New York.

Nelson, Richard & Galas, Judith (1994). **The power to prevent suicide.** Free Spirit Publishing. MN.

Poussaint, Alvin. M.D., and Alexander, Amy (2001). **Lay My Burden Down: Unraveling Suicide and the Mental Health Crisis Among African-Americans.** Beacon Press.

Robbins, Anthony (1991). **Awaken the giant within; how to take immediate control of your mental, emotional, physical & financial destiny.** Summit Books. New York.

Robinson, Rita and Hart, Phyllis (2001). **Survivors of Suicide.** New Page Books.

Rubel, Barbara (2000). **But I didn't say goodbye: for parents and professionals helping child suicide survivors.** Griefwork Center, Inc.

Smolin, Ann and Guinan, John (1993). **Healing after the suicide of a loved one.** Simon and Schuster.

Welshons, John (2003). **Awakening from grief: finding the way back to joy.** Publishers Group West. Maui, HI.

Wrobleski, Adina (2002). **Suicide of a child.** Centering Corp.

Journal

Write or draw about:

· **Any fears that you may have about uncovering the source of your pain.**

Appendix C

Suggested Reading List for Children and Teens

Cammarata, Doreen (2000). **Someone I love died by suicide: a story for child survivors and those who care for them.** Grief Guidance, Inc.

Fields, Terri (2002). **After the death of Anna Gonzales.** Henry Holt. New York.

Galas, Judith (1994). **Teen Suicide.** Thomson Gale.

Goldman, Linda (1999). **Life and loss: a guide to help grieving children.** Taylor and Francis.

Kuklin, Susan (1994). **After a suicide: young people speak up.** G.P. Putnam's Sons, New York.

Miller, Mary Beth (2002). **Aimee: a novel.** Dutton. New York.

Parkin, Rebecca and Dunne-Maxim, Karen (1995). **Child survivors of suicide: a guidebook for those who care for them.**

Ross, Eleanora Betsy et. al, (2002). **After suicide: a ray of hope for those left behind.** Perseus Publishing.

Schleifer, Jay (1993). **Everything you need to know about teen suicide.** Rosen.

Appendix D

Summaries of Books Focused on "Survivor's Stories"

Jossey-Bass, Alexander (1998). **In the wake of suicide: stories of the people left behind.**

The author spent ten years collecting stories from fellow survivors, which she compiled into this well-organized collection.

Bolton, Iris and Mitchell, Curtis (1995). **My son... my son: a guide to healing after death, loss or suicide.** The Bolton Press.

A mother's account of her progression through the grief process after the suicide of her 20-year old son.

Fine, Carla (1996). **No time to say goodbye: surviving the suicide of a loved one.**

After the suicide of her husband, the author interviewed over 100 suicide survivors. Fine weaves their experiences into her book, creating a story of loss, grief, and survival.

Glover, Beryl (2000). **The empty chair: The journey of grief after suicide.** In Sight Books.

Describes the grief process as experienced by a variety of people dealing with different emotions following the suicide of a family member.

Stimming, Mary and Maureen (1999). **Before their time: adult children's experiences of parental suicide.** Temple University Press.

Presents adult children survivors' accounts of their loss, grief, and resolution following a parent's suicide. Separate sections offer perspectives on the deaths of mothers and fathers. Also includes the reflections of four siblings on the shared loss of their mother.

Wertheimer, Alison (2001). **A special scar: the experience of people bereaved by suicide.**

The author, who lost her sister to suicide, presents interviews with fifty survivors and covers a wide range of issues, including the press, stigma, guilt, anger and rejection.

Appendix E

Suicide Crisis Lines

United States:
1-800-273-TALK or 1-800-273-8255
1-800-SUICIDE or 1-800-784-2433

Canada:
1-800-SUICIDE or 1-800-784-2433

United Kingdom:
08457 90 90 90

Republic of Ireland:
1850 90 90 90

Appendix F

Support Groups

American Association of Suicidology
5221 Wisconsin Ave., NW
Washington, DC 20015
(202) 237-2280
www.suicidology.org

Canadian Association for Suicide Prevention
c/o The Support Network
#301, 11456 Jasper Avenue
Edmonton, Alberta T5K 0M1
(780) 482-0198
www.suicideprevention.ca

Center for Attitudinal Healing
33 Buchanan Drive
Sausalito, CA 94965
(415) 331-6161
(451) 331-4545
www.attitudinalhealing.org

Compassionate Friends
The Compassionate Friends, Inc.
P.O. Box 3696
Oak Brook, IL 60522-3696
(630) 990-0010
www.compassionatefriends.org

Survivor of Suicide (S.O.S.)
Directory Of SOS Support Groups www.afsp.org/survivor/groups.htm
(888) 333-2377

Dee Burt

Appendix G

Post Traumatic Stress Symptoms (PTSD)

The following symptoms and information was taken from:
www.metanoia.org/suicide/ptsd.htm

by David L. Conroy, PhD.

Problems and symptoms include: Persistent, intrusive, and vivid memories concerning the traumatic situation. Events of daily life may trigger distressing memories related to the trauma. Memory lapses for parts of the traumatic situation. Many suicidal people are troubled by strong images, such as the feeling that they have bombs inside their bodies or a knife over their heads. During recovery they continue to be bothered by the memory of having had these images.

Some may experience:
- Avoidance of things associated with the traumatic experience.
- Denial on the seriousness of the experience.
- Persistent anxiety.
- Fear that the traumatic situation will recur. The trauma is often an event that shatters the survivors' sense of invulnerability to harm.
- Disturbing, intrusive, violent impulses and thoughts.
- Engagement in risk-taking behavior to produce adrenaline.
- A feeling of being powerless over the traumatic event. Anger and frustration over being powerless.
- A feeling of being helpless about one's current condition.
- Being dramatically and permanently changed by the experience.
- A sense of unfairness. Why did this happen to me?
- Holding one's self responsible for what happened. Feeling guilty.
- An inability to experience the joys of life.
- The use of self-blame to provide an illusion of control. Sexual assault survivors often blame themselves: "If I hadn't been at that location, worn those clothes, behaved in that way, then it wouldn't have happened." This pattern is also found in the survivors of a completed suicide. "If I had only done x, the suicide would not have happened," can be used to try to cope with the fear that suicide will happen again in the family. The suicidal are often full of self-blame. As in the other cases it is partly due to an internalization of social attitudes that blame the victim or family, and also due to the effort to gain mastery over the situation. To imagine we could have done more is more tolerable than total helplessness.

•Feelings of being alienated from the other people and society in general. "I am different. I am shameful. If they knew what I was like, they would reject me. I don't belong in this world. I'm a freak, an outcast."

When people with PTSD try to return to normal life, they are plagued by readjustment problems. They suffer from:

•Difficulties in relationships, in employment, and in having families.

•A lack of caring attachments. A sense of a lack of purpose and meaning.

•Some chronically traumatized people lose the sense that they have a self at all.

•Suicide attempters often experience great anger from family and care providers.

•A deep distrust of co-workers, employers, authorities.

In personal relationships there are problems of dependency and trust. A fear of being abandoned, betrayed, let down. A belief that people will be hurtful if given a chance. Feelings of self-hatred and humiliation for being needy, weak, and vulnerable. Alternating between isolation and anxious clinging.

•Trauma often causes the victim to view the world as malevolent, rather than benign.

•No sense of having a future, or, the belief that one's future will be very limited.

•Feel that they belong more to the dead than to the living.

•The feeling that everything I get involved with goes bad.

•Loss of self-confidence, and loss of feelings of mastery and competence.

•A resistance to efforts to change a maladaptive world view that results from the trauma.

•A mistrust of counselors' ability to listen.

People who suffered traumatic experiences as children, teenagers, or young adults may simultaneously become prematurely aged and developmentally arrested. A part of them "feels old." Another part feels stuck at the age they were when the trauma occurred.

PTSD can be worse if the sufferer experiences the trauma as an individual rather than as a member of a group of people who are suffering the same situation. Suicidal people experience their near-death situation with extreme isolation. They see their conditions as being completely unique.

Following may also be experienced:

•They have no sense of identification with others.

•The severity of PTSD symptoms tends to increase with the severity and duration of the trauma.

•The use of alcohol or drugs to cope with the PTSD symptoms.

•Attempts to do things to gain a feeling of mastery over the traumatic situation, e.g., become a volunteer on a hotline.

These kinds of conditions may be found again and again in the chronically suicidal. Upon reflection, it should not be surprising that we should suffer PTSD. Many of us suffered from suicidal pain for years. The idea of dying is terrifying. We recoil at thoughts of dying by automobile accident, plane crash, murder, cancer, AIDS, drowning, suffocation. The idea of dying violently simply by forces generated from within our selves is in some ways almost too horrible to comprehend. How could anyone survive such a prolonged siege of pain and terror and remain unaffected?

Survivors of traumatic experiences are often told, "It's in the past. Forget about it and get on with your life," "Why can't you just forget about all that, and enjoy life like a normal person?" If survivors could simply "get on with life," they would have done it. PTSD helps explain why it is so hard for the chronically suicidal to recover.

We can heal from the original trauma, and we can heal from the PTSD conditions that have plagued us since the trauma. The basic steps of PTSD recovery programs provide helpful guidelines:

- live in an environment that is physically and emotionally safe
- receive treatment for addictive behaviors
- maintain patience: PTSD recovery takes time
- nurture caring attachments
- restore sense of mastery
- get plenty of rest and relaxation
- recall the traumatic event(s) in small steps
- gradually assimilate painful feelings and memories
- fully experience fear, anger, shame, guilt, depression
- grieve one's losses

The following information was taken from the American Academy of Child & Adolescent Psychiatry website: www.aacap.org/publications/factsfam/ptsd70.htm.

A child with PTSD may also re-experience the traumatic event by:
- having frequent memories of the event, or in young children, play in which some or all of the trauma is repeated over and over
- having upsetting and frightening dreams
- acting or feeling like the experience is happening again
- developing repeated physical or emotional symptoms when the child is reminded of the event

Children with PTSD may also show the following symptoms:
- worry about dying at an early age
- losing interest in activities
- having physical symptoms such as headaches and stomachaches
- showing more sudden and extreme emotional reactions
- having problems falling or staying asleep
- demonstrating irritability or angry outbursts
- having problems concentrating
- acting younger than their age (for example, clingy or whiny behavior, thumbsucking)
- showing increased alertness to the environment
- repeating behavior that reminds them of the trauma

Appendix H

Facts about Suicide

The following facts about suicide were taken from the American Association of Suicidology (2002) (www.suicidology.org).
• More than 31,000 people die by suicide.
• An average of 87 individuals per day (one per 17 minutes) will die by suicide.
• Suicide is the 11th leading cause of death, with a rate of 11.0 per 100,000.
• Males complete suicide at a rate four times that of females; however, females attempt suicide three times more often than males.
• The suicide rates for Whites are approximately twice those of non-Whites.
• Mental health diagnoses are generally associated with a higher rate of suicide.
• The risk for suicide is increased in depressed and alcoholic individuals.
• Feelings of hopelessness are found to be more predictive of suicide risk than depression.
• The majority of individuals who are suicidal often display clues and warning signs.

Youth (ages 15-24):
• Suicide is the third leading cause of death; only accidents and homicides are more frequent.
• The 2002 rate was 9.9 suicides per 100,000 (a total of 4,010).
• One youth completes suicide every 2 hours and 11 minutes, which is about 11 each day.
• Males between the ages of 20 and 24 were 6.6 times more likely than females to complete suicide.
• Males between 15 and 19 were 6 times more likely than females to complete suicide.
• For every completed suicide by youth, it is estimated that 100 to 200 attempts are made.

Elderly (over 65):
• The elderly make up 12.3% of the population but account for 17.5% of all suicides.
• In 2001, there were 5,548 elderly suicides (about 15 per day).
• Elderly white men are at the highest risk with a rate of approximately 35 suicides per 100,000 each year.
• The rate of suicide for women declines after age 60 (after peaking in middle adulthood, ages 40-54).
• Although older adults attempt suicide less often than those in other age groups, they have a higher completion rate. Over the age of 65, there is 1 suicide for every 4 attempts.

Warning Signs:
- Hopelessness
- Rage, uncontrolled anger, seeking revenge
- Acting reckless or engaging in risky activities, seemingly without thinking
- Feeling trapped-as if there's no way out
- Increasing alcohol or drug use
- Withdrawing from friends, family, and society
- Anxiety, agitation, inability to sleep or sleeping all the time
- Dramatic mood changes
- Expressing no reason for living; no sense of purpose in life

Appendix I

Suggested Websites for Adults

www.afsp.org

www.al-anon.alateen.org

www.angelfire.com/ga4/ffos/Suicide_Discussion_Board.html

www.befrienders.org

www.compassionatefriends.org

www.forbettertimes.com

www.griefnet.org.

www.healingthehurt.com.

www.ncptsd.va.gov/faq.html (National Center for Post Traumatic Stress Disorder)

www.recovery.org/aa

www.suicide-helplines.org

www.suicideprevention.ca (Canada)

www.Suicidology.org

www.survivorsofsuicide.com

Appendix J

Frequently Asked Questions from Survivors

The following information was taken from the American Foundation for Suicide Prevention (AFSP). Additional support and information may be requested at:

AFSP
120 Wall Street
2nd Floor
New York, NY 1005
www.afsp.org
1-888-333-AFSP

Why did this happen? 90 percent of all people who die by suicide have a diagnosable psychiatric disorder at the time of their death (most often depression or bipolar disorder). Many survivors struggle to understand the reasons for the suicide, asking themselves over and over again: "Why?"

Many replay their loved ones, last days, searching for clues, particularly if they didn't see any signs that suicide was imminent. Just as people can die of heart disease or cancer, people can die as a consequence of mental illness. Suicide is almost always complicated and is the result of a combination of painful suffering, desperate hopelessness, and underlying psychiatric illness.

What could I have done? Psychologists Bob Baugher and Jack Jordan explain, "Once a person has decided to end his or her life, there are limits to how much anyone can do to stop the act. People sometimes find a way to kill themselves when hospitalized on locked psychiatric units under careful supervision. Be realistic about how preventable the suicide was and how much you could have done to intervene. On some level, your loved one made a choice to end his or her suffering through suicide.

Medical research is also demonstrating that major psychiatric disorders involve changes in the functioning of the brain that can severely alter the thinking, mood, and behavior of someone suffering from the disorder. This means that while stress, social problems, and other environmental factors can contribute to the development of a psychiatric disorder, the illness produces biological changes in the individual that create the emotional and physical pain (depression, inabilities to take pleasure in things, hopelessness, etc.) which contribute to almost all suicides."

What do I do now?

Some survivors struggle with what to tell other people. Usually it is best to simply acknowledge that their loved one died by suicide. You may find that it helps to reach out to family and friends. Because some people may not know what to say, you may need to take the initiative to talk about the suicide, share your feelings, and ask for their help. Each person grieves in his or her own way. Some people visit the cemetery weekly; others find it too painful to go at all.

Some things that may comfort you are:

• Maintain contact with other people.

• Many survivors use the arts to help them heal, by keeping a journal, or writing poetry or music.

• Take care of your own well-being; consider visiting your doctor for a check-up.

• Remember, all of your feelings are normal.

• Anger, guilt, confusion, forgetfulness are common responses. You are not crazy. You are in mourning.

• Be aware you may feel appropriate anger at the person, at the world, at God, at yourself. It's okay to express it.

• You may feel guilty for what you think you did or did not do. Guilt can turn into regret through forgiveness.

• Having suicidal thoughts is common. It does not mean that you will act on those thoughts.

• Remember to take one moment or one day at a time.

• Find a good listener with whom to share. Call someone if you need to talk.

• Don't be afraid to cry. Tears are healing.

• Give yourself time to heal.

• Remember, the choice was not yours. No one is the sole influence in another's life.

• Expect setbacks. If emotions return like a tidal wave, you may only be experiencing a remnant of grief, an unfinished piece.

• Try to put off major decisions.

• Give yourself permission to get professional help.

• Be aware of the pain of your family and friends.

• Be patient with yourself and with others who may not understand.

• Set your own limits and learn to say no.

• Give yourself space and steer clear of people who want to tell you what or how to feel.

• Know that there are support groups that can be helpful. If you can't find one, ask a professional to help start one.

• Call on your personal faith to help you through.

• It is common to experience physical reactions to your grief, such as headaches, loss of appetite, inability to sleep.

•The willingness to laugh with others and at yourself is healing.

•Wear out all your questions, anger, guilt or other feelings until you can let them go. Letting go doesn't mean forgetting.

How should I handle the holidays? Do what you think will be comfortable for you. Remember, you can always choose to do things differently next time.

•Family members may feel differently about continuing to do things the way they've been done in the past. Try to talk openly with each other about your expectations.

•Consider whether you want to be with your family and friends for the holiday, or whether it would be more healing for you to be by yourself or take a little vacation.

•Sometimes the anticipation of an event can be more difficult than the event itself.

•If you find it comforting to talk about your loved one, let your family and friends know that; tell them not to be afraid to mention your loved one's name.

•Acknowledge the birthday of loved ones by gathering with his/her friends and family; or you may prefer to spend it privately.

Some survivors have found the following ritual helpful for a variety of occasions:

•Light two candles, and then blow one out. Explain that the extinguished candle represents those we've lost, while the one that continues to burn represents those of us who go on despite our loss and pain.

How do we help children cope? Children are particularly vulnerable to feeling abandoned and guilty. Listen to their questions, and try to offer honest, straightforward, age-appropriate answers.

Here are some suggestions from **Child Survivors of Suicide: A Guidebook for Those Who Care for Them**, by Rebecca Parkin and Karen Dunne-Maxim about how to explain the death to children:

•When you have a choice, tell them as soon as you have the news, in a place where both you and they will feel comfortable.

•Reassure them that the death was not their fault.

•Explain that their loved one died of an illness for example, a brain illness.

•Resist the urge to keep the suicide a secret out of fear that the child will copy the behavior of the deceased.

•Reassure children that you and your family and friends will take care of them. Let them know they can approach you at any time if they want to talk about it. Children may express their feelings by crying, withdrawing, laughing, or expressing anger at you or others. Let them know you are available for whatever they need now or at some later time.

•Resume and maintain the child's regular routine as much as possible. The greatest gift you can give children is your assurance of love and support. Allow them to express their feelings, answer their questions and provide them with affection.

How can friends of survivors help?

Honor and respect the needs of the survivors in the days, weeks and months following the suicide.

The following guidelines from The Link Counseling Center's National Resource Center for Suicide Prevention and Aftercare will help you understand what may be comforting to the family. Always ask survivors whether they need your help. Some survivors gain added strength from performing many of the responsibilities listed below, while others may want to rely on friends or family for support and guidance.

•Respond honestly to questions asked by the family. You don't need to answer more than asked. If they want to know more, they will ask later.

•Surround them with as much love and understanding as you can.

•Give them some private time. Be there, but don't smother them. Show love, not control.

•Let them talk. Most of the time they just need to hear out loud what is going on inside their heads. They usually aren't seeking advice.

•Encourage the idea that decisions should be made by the family together.

•Expect that they will become tired easily. Grieving is hard work.

•Let them decide what they are ready for. Offer your ideas but let them decide themselves.

•Keep a list of phone calls, visitors and people who bring food and gifts.

•Offer to make calls to people they wish to notify.

•Keep the mail straight. Keep track of bills, cards, newspaper notices, appointments, etc.

•Help with errands.

•Keep a list of medication administered.

•Offer to help with documentation needed by the insurance company, such as a copy of the death certificate.

•Give special attention to members of the family at the funeral and in the months to come.

•Allow them to express as much grief as they are feeling at the moment and are willing to share.

•Allow them to talk about the special endearing qualities of the loved one they have lost.

Bibliography

Bradshaw, John (1992). Creating love: the next great stage of growth. Bantam Books: New York.

Bradshaw, John (1995). Family Secrets: what you don't know can hurt you. Bantam Books: New York.

Bradshaw, John (1988), Healing the shame that binds you. Health Communications.

Brenner, Anne (1994). Mourning & mitzvah: a guided journal for walking the mourner's path through grief to healing.

Emerson, Ralph Waldo (1951). Essays by Ralph Waldo Emerson: first and second series complete in one volume. The Borgo Press: San Bernardino.

Epictetus, (1995). The art of living: the classical manual on virtue, happiness, and effectiveness. Harper: San Francisco.

Jampolsky, Gerald (1979). Love is letting go of fear. Celestial Arts. CA

Jampolsky, Gerald (1983). Teach only love; the principles of attitudinal healing. Bantam Books, New York.

Kubler-Ross, Elisabeth (1975). Death the final stage of growth. Prentice-Hall. New Jersey.

Kubler-Ross, Elisabeth (1970). On death and dying. Macmillan, New York.

Levine, Stephen (1991). Guided meditations, explorations and healings. Doubleday: New York.

Lewis, C.S. (1994). A grief observed. Harper, San Francisco.

Lucas, C. & Seiden, H. (1987). Silent grief: living in the wake of suicide. Scribner's: New York.

O'Neill, Nena (2004). Stand up for your life: one woman's journey through cancer.

Peck, Scott & Shannon (1999). Liberating your magnificence: 25 keys to loving & healing yourself. Lifepath Publications.

Trout, Susan (1990). To see differently: personal growth and being of service through attitudinal healing. Aladdin Books.

Viorst, Judith (1986). Necessary losses. Simon and Schuster. New York.

Dee Burt

About the Author

Dee Burt earned her Master of Science in Education with her area of concentration in Counseling and Educational Psychology. She began journaling to help deal with the aftermath of her husband's suicide during the first few semesters of her undergraduate coursework.

Dee presents loss and grief workshops focusing on the messages within each individual and the healing power those messages provide.

Dee presents writing workshops and professional development seminars for schools utilizing bibliotherapeutic strategies to engage children and adults in writing and celebrating a wide range of stories and experiences.

Dee and her husband, Paul, founded Pen & Publish, Inc. to support schools, churches and nonprofits in providing beneficial educational and emotional health building writing and publication opportunities.

Contact Dee Burt at OneSide@penandpublish.com